Mastering the German Case System:

Nominative, Accusative, Dative & Genitive

with Herr Antrim

If you would like to receive free German lessons, motivation and tips sent via email on a regular basis, join Herr Antrim's newsletter at https://www.germanwithantrim.com/

Thank you for choosing this book. If you have some spare time, consider writing a review online. If you want to write a review on Amazon, you can use this link: https://www.germanwithantrim.com/mastering-cases-review/

Contents

How to Use This Book

Each chapter of this book is dedicated to a particular lesson or group of lessons. Each chapter includes additional materials such as online flashcards and mp3 downloads of example sentences as well as practice exercises (worksheets) and answer keys for each.

You can find these worksheets, answer keys and more in Herr Antrim's "Deutschlerner Club", which includes explanation videos to go with each worksheet at https://www.germanwithantrim.com/store/

Alternatively you can purchase the companion workbook wherever you purchased this book or download and print your own worksheets via the links provided throughout the book. To purchase the workbook on Amazon go to https://www.germanwithantrim.com/mastering-cases-workbook-paperback/

Start by reading a section of a chapter and trying to understand what is being taught. Listen to the audio of the example sentences via the links provided at the end of each chapter. Try to repeat the examples to practice pronunciation and to solidify the concept.

Once you think you have a good grasp of the information in that section, try the worksheet(s) that go with that part of the chapter. Each section of the chapter are labeled in the workbook and worksheets so you can complete one part of the chapter at a time.

It is not recommended that you do all of the worksheets for one whole chapter all at once. Pace yourself and make sure you understand one concept before moving on to the next.

Check your answers with the answer key(s) provided or the video explanations in the Deutschlerner Club. Use the online flashcards to review the words and phrases that you learned in that lesson. Re-read or re-listen to the lesson again in a day or so. This will help you to store the information in your long-term memory.

Throughout this book you will notice two patterns. The first is a color code of cases within example sentences. The color coding is meant to help you internalize the case system. The more you encounter it, the more you see the nominative case things written in red, the more you will see the location of these words and associate the placement, color and case all together. Do this for all of the cases and you will be on your way to mastering this system that much faster.

In addition to the color code, there are a number of charts throughout this book. They always use the same order for the articles. This order is listed below along with the color coordination.

Cases Color Code

Nominative
Accusative
Dative
Genitive

Chart Order

Masculine	Feminine	Neuter	Plural

we are on the topic of "the order of things", now would be an opportune time to mention that German (and most Latin-based languages) usually do not list the cases in the order that I do in this book.

I list them as nominative, accusative, dative and genitive, because this is the order in which most English native speakers learn about the cases. It is the order they show up in most textbooks. It follows the general order of easiest to most complicated, although I would argue that the genitive case is easier than the dative.

German native speakers and many grammar nerds will list the cases in the order of nominative, genitive, dative, accusative. Sometimes they go as far as to number them: 1. Fall - Nominativ, 2. Fall - Genitiv, 3. Fall - Dativ, 4. Fall - Akkusativ. (The German word for "case", by the way" is "Fall" and the dot behind the number indicates things like -st and -nd making numbers "ordinal numbers" like first, second, third and fourth.)

Additional Resources

Deutschlerner Club:
Every lesson within this book is also available as part of Herr Antrim's Deutschlerner Club. This is an online subscription that grants you access to the A1 and A2 courses as well as lessons Herr Antrim uploads to his YouTube channel. Since the publication of this book there is now an additional course in the Deutschlerner Club designed to follow this book and provide even more support for your mastery of the German case system. You can get free samples of the Deutschlerner Club or join here:
https://www.germanwithantrim.com/store/

Companion Workbook:
Practice what you learn in this book with worksheets and answer keys designed to follow this book exactly so you make sure you actually master everything you learn here. Look for Herr Antrim's companion workbook wherever books are sold.

Online Flashcards:

Flashcards that include example sentences with audio, verb lists, and general vocabulary covered throughout this book can be found in the flashcards folder at

https://www.germanwithantrim.com/mastering-cases/

These flashcards are built on the Anki platform, but should be easy to import into your flashcard app of choice.

Email Support:

I love hearing from my fans (and occasionally from my critics). If you have questions about the book, how to use it to get the best results, where to find any of the materials, or anything you want to know, send me an email at info@germanwithantrim.com

If you find an error in these pages, please send me an email about that too. I want this book to be the best resource it can be for German learners and while I did have a few native speakers read through this book before publishing it, there is always a chance that something slipped by the censors.

What are grammatical cases?

According to Wikipedia a grammatical case is:

> *a special grammatical category of a noun, pronoun, adjective, participle or numeral whose value reflects the grammatical function performed by that word in a phrase, clause or sentence*

This is a horrendous definition. It is too long, includes a ton of grammatical jargon that no one understands, and to any normal person, it makes no sense. This is usually the first problem with many language courses. They assume that everyone is an academic or a grammar nerd. Most people, however, are neither of those things. Let's try and simplify this a bit.

My definition would be as follows:

> *a way to identify what a noun or pronoun*
> *(and the stuff that goes with them) is doing in a particular sentence.*

I used the least amount of grammatical jargon as possible and, as with any jargon I mention throughout this book, I will define what they mean so everyone can understand.

Nouns are people, places and things. Most teachers include the word "ideas" on the list of what a noun is, but, in my mind, ideas are things, which makes this inclusion a bit extra.

Pronouns are generally shorter words that replace nouns. Sometimes they are used to replace a specific noun. For example: We can replace "the table" with "it" in English rather than using the word "table" every time.

In other situations, pronouns are simply used to avoid speaking in the third person, like Elmo. "Elmo loves playing games." Elmo should say "I like playing games." "I" is a pronoun.

What Grammatical Cases Do in German?

In German, because of the case system, it is grammatically acceptable to move around word order without affecting the meaning of a sentence. Take the following sentence as an example.

Der Mann gibt dem Jungen einen Lutscher. -
The man gives the boy a lollipop.

The man is the one doing something in the sentence. We call this the subject. The subject in English is almost always first. In German we identify the subject through the use of the nominative case in addition to the word order.

If you move the word order around in English, things get confusing. In German you can start sentences with pretty much anything you want with very few exceptions, because of the case system. You could rewrite the same sentence like this.

Einen Lutscher gibt der Mann dem Jungen. -
The man gives the boy a lollipop.

In this version, I started the sentence with the direct object. That is the thing that is being acted upon. In other words, it is the thing being given in the sentence. Thanks to the German case system, the meaning of the sentence did not change. The man is still the one giving something and the something given is still the lollipop. The accusative case is used to identify the direct object in German.

The only thing that really changed is that the emphasis of the sentence has changed from the subject, the man, to the direct object, the lollipop. The only way to do this in English is to use your voice to put emphasis on the word "lollipop". "The man gives the boy **a lollipop**."

You can also start a sentence with the indirect object, the one receiving the direct object. In the next example you can see that "dem Jungen" is first, which, thanks to the case system, is still receiving the lollipop that the man is giving. Again, the English equivalent would require you to add emphasis using your voice. You would say,

The man gives **the boy** a lollipop.

Dem Jungen gibt der Mann einen Lutscher. -
The man gives the boy a lollipop.

The words "der", "dem" and "einen" in the examples above help to identify how the words that follow them are being used within the sentence. This is the purpose of the case system in German.

While you can change the emphasis within the sentence with your voice, as you do in English, it is also possible to emphasize various parts of the sentence by moving them around within the sentence. Usually this is done by moving the emphasized thing to the beginning of the sentence. Other times it is done by moving something closer to the verb. The case system makes all of these word order changes possible.

It should be noted that the examples I gave, with the exception of the "regular word order example" are not common. The way the word order changes in conversations usually involves moving the time to the beginning of the sentence or putting a prepositional phrase in front.

Prepositions are little words that are used with nouns or pronouns to add extra context to the sentence. The preposition plus the noun or pronoun used with it make up a prepositional phrase. These are covered extensively throughout this book.

The bottom line is that the case system makes it easier to identify how a word is being used within the sentence, so the sentence as a whole can be more easily understood. As with any grammatical structure in any language, the purpose is communication. The case system in German makes communication more efficient and effective.

An Introduction to
German Noun Genders

Every German noun has a grammatical gender assigned to it. These genders help the case system function in a meaningful way. While cases do not necessitate genders nor vice versa, they do work together incredibly well.

Sometimes this gender reflects the intrinsic gender of the person or animal to which it refers. For example: "Mann" means "man" and is a masculine noun. "Frau" means "woman" and is a feminine noun. "Fenster" means "window" and is a neuter noun.

♂ der Mann - the man   der Löffel - the spoon
♀ die Frau - the woman   die Gabel - the fork
♀ das Fenster - the window   das Messer - the knife

More often than not, it is less obvious why a noun has a particular gender. For example: der Löffel (spoon), die Gabel (fork) and das Messer (knife). There is no logical reasoning for why a spoon is masculine, a fork is feminine and a knife is neuter. They just are, because grammatical gender is a mysterious thing that doesn't follow many rules. (Although I will show you some rules in the next chapter.) This is the reason you should always memorize the gender of the noun when you learn new vocabulary by including "der", "die", or "das" with the noun.

This is not to say that "der" is always masculine or "die" is always feminine. We use the articles "der", "die" and "das" as placeholders to remind you that the noun is masculine, feminine or neuter.

To identify these genders within sentences we use a variety of articles and word endings. Articles can be words for "the", called definite articles, or words for "a/an", called indefinite articles. The default definite article form is the nominative case. In that case, "der" is used to identify masculine nouns, "die" for feminine and "das" for neuter.

It is important to understand that "der", "die", and "das" are not accurate ways to describe the genders of nouns in German. They are simply labels for genders that are built into the nouns. This is important for several reasons, but the biggest one is that "der" isn't always masculine. In the dative and genitive cases "der" is used before feminine and plural nouns.

A quick side note here: in addition to the masculine, feminine and neuter genders, there are also articles associated with the plural forms of nouns. While these articles are the same as the feminine for the first two cases in this book (nominative and accusative), they are different in the dative and genitive cases.

For example: die Kinder (children) is the plural form of the noun in the nominative and accusative cases. When we get to the dative case it becomes "den Kindern", which not only changed the article from "die" to "den", but also added an -n to the end of the noun. While in English "die Kinder", "den Kindern" and "der Kinder" all translate as "the children", it is important to know how the word is being used within the sentence in German, as this will decide which form of the noun we need.

These grammatical genders are not without their purpose. When combined with the grammatical case system, we can easily identify the way in which a word is being used within the sentence. This makes it easier to understand at a glance, even if the word order is switched up.

For example: "You are buying it." in English is very different than "It is buying you."

You are buying it. ≠ It is buying you.
Du kaufst ihn. = Ihn kaufst du.

In German, however, "Du kaufst ihn." is the same as "Ihn kaufst du.", as "du" indicates the subject (one doing the action) and "ihn" indicates the direct object (one being acted upon).

Er kauft ihn. -
He is buying it.

Ihn kauft er. -
He is buying it.

These examples show the same expression, but one starts with the subject (the one buying something) and the other starts with the direct object (the thing being bought). We know which is which because of the case system.

**Der Mann kauft den Mantel. -
The man is buying the coat.**

We can tell that "der Mann" is the subject of the German sentence, because it uses the article "der", which indicates a masculine noun that is the subject of the sentence. "den Mantel", by contrast, is also a masculine noun, but it uses the article "den" to show us that it is the thing being bought.

Even if we switched the word order and said "Den Mantel kauft der Mann.", we could still tell that the man is the one doing something, because it used the article "der". In English "the man" doesn't tell us right away that he is the subject. The German gender and case system helps us be flexible.

The articles and pronouns don't always change, however, between the subject and object cases. This is most notable with feminine nouns. When this happens, the sentence becomes reliant on word order, just like we do in English.

**Die Frau kauft die Bluse. -
The woman is buying the blouse.**

This time we can't switch the word order without making the blouse sentient. Let's be honest, no one wants to live in a world where a blouse goes shopping for a woman. It would make a decent episode of the *Twilight Zone*, however.

It becomes even more confusing, when you change out the nouns for pronouns, as both "die Frau" and "die Bluse" would use the article "sie" in German. This makes our sentence:

**Sie kauft sie. -
She is buying it.**

The bottom line is that we need the case system to make the language more efficient and effective and we need the genders of nouns to help use this case system.

Grammatical Gender Tips and Tricks

In the German language, understanding the gender of nouns is not optional. It lays the foundation for everything from grammar and vocabulary building to making sure that you are understood and can communicate effectively. It is the key that unlocks the door to fluency and accurate communication. Understanding this concept is crucial for anyone learning German, as it affects almost every aspect of the language.

Learning noun genders might seem daunting, but with practice, it becomes second nature. Always learn nouns with their articles and look for patterns and rules that can guide you. I'll teach you some of these patterns and rules in this chapter.

As we progress, keep in mind that understanding noun genders is more than just memorization. It's about understanding the rhythm and flow of the German language.

Masculine Nouns

Let's start with masculine nouns. Certain categories of nouns are always masculine. This includes male people and animals, days of the week, months, seasons, and weather phenomena.

People	Animals	Days of the Week
der Mann	der Hund	der Montag
der Lehrer	der Kater	der Dienstag
der Arzt	der Löwe	der Mittwoch
der Bauer	der Bär	der Donnerstag
der Anwalt	der Hahn	der Freitag
der Polizist	der Elefant	der Samstag
der Koch	der Hai	der Sonntag

Weather		
der Schnee	der Nebel	der Niederschlag
der Regen	der Hagel	der Wind

Months		Seasons
der Januar	Juli	der Winter
der Februar	August	der Frühling
der März	September	der Sommer
der April	Oktober	der Herbst
der Mai	November	
der Juni	Dezember	

Let's look at some specific examples. The most obvious use for the masculine gender of nouns is for male people and animals. This includes not only the on-the-nose example of "der Mann" (the man), but also pretty much every occupation there is. For a male person in that profession, there is a masculine word with a masculine gender and a masculine article to match. The same is true for female people. "Der Lehrer" is masculine while "die Lehrerin" is feminine. Both translate as "teacher" in English which is ambiguous.

The same rule can be applied to most, but strangely not all animals. There is "der Hund" for male dogs and "die Hündin" for female dogs. "der Kater" for a male cat and "die Katze" for the female cat. "Der Löwe" and "die Löwin" for lion and lioness respectively.

Be careful with this generalization with animals, however, as there are lots of examples of animals that don't follow this convention. For example: das Pferd (horse), das Zebra (zebra), das Huhn (chicken), and das Faultier (sloth), just to name a few.

Without going too far into the examples for later in this chapter, Almost all baby animals and even baby humans are neuter. This includes: das Baby (baby), das Lamm (lamb), das Kalb (calf), das Fohlen (foal), and das Küken (chick) and a whole lot more. There are, of course, exceptions to this rule as well. Most notably "der Welpe" for puppy.

Days of the week, months, seasons and directions on a compass are all masculine. Luckily there are no exceptions to this rule, but there are a few people feverishly writing in an Amazon review for this book that the word "das Frühjahr" exists as an alternative to "der Frühling" for spring and you can refer to the rainy season as "die Regenzeit" and the dry season as "die Trockenzeit". Ironically, the word for season is also not masculine. It is "die Jahreszeit".

Outside of those pedantic examples, this rule works every time.

der Montag (Monday), der Dienstag (Tuesday), der Mittwoch (Wednesday), der Januar (January), der Februar (Feburary), der März (March), der Winter (Winter), der Herbst (Fall), der Sommer (Summer), der Norden (North), der Süden (South), der Westen (West).

I mentioned also that most weather phenomena are masculine, but there are plenty of exceptions to this. Most precipitation, however, is safely assumed to be masculine. For example: der Regen (rain), der Hagel (hail), der Schnee (snow), and der Nebel (fog).

Certain word endings typically signify a masculine noun. These include -ismus (der Tourismus - tourism), -ig (der Honig - honey), -or (der Motor - motor) and -ling (der Schmetterling - butterfly).

Some blogs contend that -er is a masculine suffix, but words like "die Mutter" (mother) and "die Schwester" (sister) make this rule difficult to take seriously. I did find one post that said -er is a masculine suffix, but that it isn't always being used as a suffix.

This basically says the same thing I was about to, which is, -er usually indicates a male person and when it doesn't, you can either go with the gender of the person or guess masculine. Just know that even then you won't be 100% correct every time.

One last group that is always masculine is cars. Specifically name brands of cars. If you say you drive a BMW car, that is "der BMW". It is also "der Mercedes", "der Audi", "der Ford" and so on. Just be careful, as the most common word for a car is neuter, "das Auto".

While these rules are helpful, remember that there are always exceptions in the German language. Some nouns might not fit the general pattern, so always check with a dictionary, if you are unsure.

Feminine Nouns

Now let's move on to feminine nouns and the article "die". Just as with masculine nouns, the most obvious category works as intended, most of the time. Female people are described using feminine nouns and female animals are described with the same.

The most notable exception to this is the noun "Mädchen", which means "girl". This is because -chen and -lein are diminutives. This is a fancy way of saying that they make things smaller and generally cuter. This was done with the word "die Magd" (maid) to make the word "Mädchen" for girl. While it would make sense to assume that the word for girl is feminine, it is actually "das Mädchen", because of the ending -chen.

die Magd + -chen = **das Mädchen**

Many internet pseudo-intellectuals like to say that this is offensive and weird, as there is no male equivalent, but this is simply not true. "der Mann" can become both "das Männchen" or "das Männlein". Both of these words mean "little man".

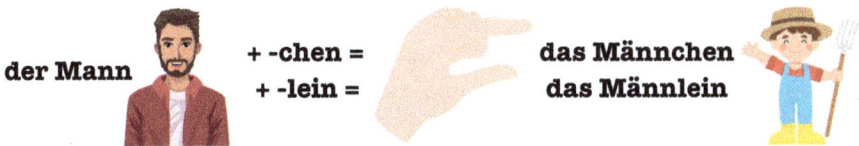

der Mann + -chen =   **das Männchen**
+ -lein =   **das Männlein**

So why isn't the German word for boy neuter in the same way? This is because it is essentially an adjective (word that describes a noun) that we pretend is a noun. "Der junge Mann" would be "the young man" in German. Eventually "der junge Mann" just became "der Junge" for boy.

der junge Mann - Mann = **der Junge**

So what about the word "Fräulein" (young lady)? Why isn't that used outside of World War 2 movies? This is because there is a perfectly good word for woman. Calling a grown person "Fräulein" would grammatically make them smaller and cuter. This is never done to men. If you were to refer to a man as "Männlein" or "Männchen" it would be equally as insulting and inappropriate. There is no alternative word for "Mädchen". It is THE word for girl.

While this argument is one way of looking at it, the other way is more likely. There used to be a need to know if a woman was married or not, because a man could not court a woman who was already married. There was a societal process that needed to be followed. As this process faded, so did the need and therefore the use of the word "Fräulein". It is the same reason I don't know anyone in the USA who goes by "Miss So-and-so" unless they really want to be courted or they want to draw attention to their divorce.

Now that I have my mini-rant out of the way, let's go back to rules that indicate feminine nouns. Most people who are feminine use feminine nouns to describe themselves. Simply add -in to the end of the male occupation name and you get the female version. For example:

Male	Female	Male	Female
der Lehrer	die Lehrerin	der Arzt	die Ärztin
der Bauer	die Bäuerin	der Anwalt	die Anwältin
der Polizist	die Polizistin	der Koch	die Köchin

You may have also noticed that when there is a good place to put an umlaut, that changes too for the female version. This is a sort of pronunciation helper to go with the addition of -in to the noun.

This same trick can be used with a lot of animal names, too. For example:

Male	Female	Male	Female
der Hund	die Hündin	der Bär	die Bärin
der Löwe	die Löwin	der Wolf	die Wölfin

There are lots of female occupations and animals, however, that do not follow this convention. For example:

Male	Female	Male	Female
der Hahn	die Henne	der Kater	die Katze

While name brands of cars are masculine, name brands of motorcycles are feminine. That means a BMW car is "der BMW", but a BMW motorcycle is "die BMW". Generally, ships are feminine, too. "die Titanic", "die Eisenhower" and "die Hamburg".

The list of suffixes for feminine nouns is incredibly helpful, as there are several endings that always, without exception, indicate a feminine noun.

These include: -heit (die Gesundheit - health), -keit (die Gemütlichkeit - coziness), -tät (die Universität - university), -ung (die Bildung - education), -schaft (die Mannschaft - team) and -tion (die Nation - nation).

-heit	-keit	-tät
die Gesundheit	die Gemütlichkeit	die Universität

-ung	-schaft	-tion
die Bildung	die Mannschaft	die Nation

A cool thing about all of those nouns, is that nouns in these groups that can have a plural form do so by adding -en at the end. die Freiheit - die Freiheiten (freedom), die Aktivität - die Aktivitäten (activity), die Beobachtung - die Beobachtungen (observation), die Freundschaft - die Freundschaften (friendship), die Funktion - die Funktionen (function).

There are lots of other suffixes that can reasonably be assumed to be feminine, but they aren't reliable enough for me to include them with one exception. About 90% of nouns that end with -e are feminine. Keep in mind, however, that this only applies to nouns that are not referring to masculine people, as those would obviously require the masculine gender.

Singular	Plural	Singular	Plural
die Tasche	die Taschen	die Lupe	die Lupen
die Note	die Noten	die Rose	die Rosen
die Klasse	die Klassen	die Schule	die Schulen

Another good rule of thumb here is that nouns that end with -e will take an -n for the plural.

Neuter Nouns

Now let's move on to the last grammatical gender, neuter, which is usually indicated by the article "das".

I already mentioned the suffixes -chen and -lein, which automatically require the grammatical gender to be neuter. I talked about it with people, however. They can also be applied to other nouns.

Original	Diminutive	Original	Diminutive
der Baum	das Bäumchen	der Hahn	das Hähnchen

Besides these two endings, you can also rely on -ment (das Instrument - instrument), and -tum (das Eigentum - property) to be neuter nouns.

das Baby	das Kind	das Kätzchen	das Lamm	das Kalb

I also said that babies for both humans and animals are usually neuter. For example: das Baby (baby), das Kind (child), das Kätzchen (the kitten), das Lamm (lamb) and das Kalb (calf).

-ment	-tum
das Instrument	das Eigentum

As with almost all rules in German, there are exceptions in neuter nouns. It's important to be aware of these and learn them as you encounter them.

Exceptions and Special Cases

Once you get the general rules down, it is time to get into some weird things that happen with German nouns. The most irritating to German learners is that there are often multiple nouns that have different genders, but the same spelling of the noun. This means that given the article in front of a noun, the meaning might be different than expected.

There are three words in German spelled B-A-N-D. "der Band" is a volume, as in a book within a series. "das Band, however, is ribbon. Then there is the word "die Band", which is the group of musicians, which is an English loan word and keeps it English-like pronunciation (die Bänd).

der Band   das Band   die Band

While "die Band" is its own word, "der Band" and "das Band" are connected, because books are bound and "Band" comes from "binden" (to bind).

There is also "der Kiefer", which means jawbone and "die Kiefer", which is a pine tree.

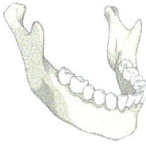

der Kiefer

die Kiefer

While I would love to tell you that this is a rare occurrence, wiktionary.org lists over 1600 of words like this.

Compound Nouns

One quirk that is actually helpful is that the genders of compound nouns are determined by the last component of the compound. For example, "das Rathaus" (town hall) is neuter because "das Haus" (house) is neuter. The fact that "Rat" (advice) is masculine does not matter.

der Rat + **das Haus** = **das Rathaus**

This means that when you see the monstrosity of "Rindfleischetikettierungsüberwachungsaufgabenübertragungsgesetz", you can take solace in the fact that "Gesetz" is neuter, so the whole word is neuter.

**das
Rindfleischetikettierungsüberwachungsaufgabenübertragungsgesetz**

das   **die**   **die**   **die**   **die**   **das**

Breaking apart long German words is an art form. This particular one is made up of lots of nouns, but if you know the pieces that make it, you can figure it out. "Das Rindfleisch" is beef, so this has something to do with that. It ends with "Gesetz" (law), so we know it is a law about beef. In all it is a law about labeling beef products.

When it comes to exceptions and special cases with regards to German noun genders, practice and exposure are your best friends. The more you read, listen, and speak in German, the more familiar you'll become with these peculiarities. With enough practice and exposure, you will be able to develop your own "Sprachgefühl" (intuitive feeling for the language), which will help you to more naturally choose the correct article for the correct noun in the correct situation.

To truly master noun genders, integrate them into your daily practice. Label objects around you in German, including their article and the plural form of the noun. Engage in conversations or write sentences using these nouns.

Now to make sure you were paying attention for the past few pages, go to chapter 1 of the workbook or visit the link below and complete the worksheets for this chapter.

You can even use the worksheet pages as a sort of cheatsheet for later when you want to remember which endings indicate which gender.

Extra materials for this chapter:
https://www.germanwithantrim.com/mastering-cases/

Nominative Case

Now that we have our base knowledge about the case system and grammatical genders, let's get into the real purpose of this book, understanding when and how to use the cases themselves.

The first case German students encounter is the nominative case. This is basically a default form of everything. When you first learn new words or you find something in a dictionary, the nominative case is the one shown.

As I mentioned in examples in the first two chapters, the nominative case is used for the subject of the sentence, which is the person or thing doing something within the sentence.

The subject is also the thing that determines how the verb is conjugated. Conjugation is the change that occurs with a verb to make sure that it matches the subject of the sentence. If you were to say something like "I goes to the store.", you are either Ralph from *The Simpsons* or you would just be grammatically incorrect.

Definite Articles

The first thing you need to learn about the nominative case is the concept of definite articles. These words are generally translated as "the" in English and they identify a specific object. Not just "any book", but "the book". The words for these are the same as what we use in German for demonstrative and relative pronouns, which are explained later in this book.

In the nominative case, masculine nouns use the article "der" to say "the". Feminine and plural use "die" and neuter nouns use "das". You can see those in the first of many charts in this book shown below.

	Masculine	Feminine	Neuter	Plural
Nominative	der	die	das	die

If you use the last letter of each of these words, you get the mnemonic "RESE" (pronounced "ressa" or "reesie"). I'll use a similar mnemonic device for all of the other definite articles in the other cases throughout this book.

♂ de**r Mann - the man**
♀ di**e Frau - the woman**
♀ da**s Fenster - the window**
⊗di**e Kinder - the children**

There are also words that act like definite articles in German. These words include: dieser (this, these, that, those), jeder (every), jener (that), (manche (some), solche (such, that kind of), welcher (which), beide (both) and alle (all).

They serve a similar function to that of the definite articles and the last letters of these words will match those of the definite articles. These words together with the definite articles are sometimes called "der-words". This is because of the masculine nominative form being "der" and also, because it is less intimidating than calling them definite articles.

When I reference "der-words" throughout the rest of this book, what I mean by that is all of the words in the definite articles chart plus the forms of "dieser", "jeder", "jener", "manche", "solche", "welcher", "beide" and "alle" that would be in the same chart.

	Masculine	Feminine	Neuter	Plural
Nominative	de**r**	di**e**	da**s**	di**e**
Nominative	diese**r**	dies**e**	diese**s**	dies**e**

**Der Mann fährt schnell. -
The man drives fast.**

In this sentence, we can tell that the man is the one doing the driving on a number of levels. The most obvious is some simple logic. Obviously the man is the only person or thing within the sentence that is capable of driving. Beyond that, we can look to the article "der" to tell us that the man is the subject.

The conjugation of the verb "fährt" also shows us that the man is the subject, because this is the "er, sie, es" or "he, she, it" form of the verb "fahren" (to drive). Also, the only other thing in the sentence is the word "schnell", which is an adverb that tells us how the man is driving. Adverbs can't be the subject of the sentence. Adverbs are words that describe the action within the sentence or words that describe adjectives (words that describe nouns).

Die Frau arbeitet fleißig. -
The woman works diligently.

"Die Frau" is the subject of this sentence, which puts her in the nominative case. We can see that through the word order (the subject is usually first in German statements). The conjugation of the verb shows a -t at the end, which again shows us the third person singular form (he, she, it form) of the verb. Of course, "fleißig" is another adverb and cannot be the subject of the sentence.

Das Fenster ist kaputt. -
The window is broken.

The window is the subject in this one, because it is the one doing something, namely "being". The word order shows us this is likely the subject and the conjugation of the verb, again, has the "er, sie, es" (he, she, it) form. "Kaputt" is another adverb telling us "how" the window is being.

Die Kinder tanzen. -
The children are dancing.

The children are plural, which is why our verb ends with -en instead of a -t like it did in all of the other examples so far. The word order and the conjugation tell us the children are the subject and therefore have to be used with the nominative case.

Now let's look at the same examples with some of those "additional der-words" I mentioned before.

Dieser Mann fährt schnell. -
This man drives fast.

This shows us the der-word "dieser" with an -er at the end to show the subject "Mann" in the nominative case.

**Jede Frau arbeitet fleißig. -
Every woman works diligently.**

Here we have the der-word "jeder" with an -e at the end to show "Frau" is the subject through word order and the ending.

**Dieses Fenster ist kaputt. -
This window is broken.**

The -es at the end of "dieses" shows us the gender of the window and the word order shows us that this window is in the nominative case as the subject.

**Diese Kinder tanzen. -
These children are dancing.**

This one requires an -e at the end of "alle" to show that the children are plural.

Complete workbook section 2.1 before continuing.

Indefinite Articles

In addition to the definite articles (words for "the"), there are also indefinite articles in German. These are generally words that translate as "a" or "an" in English. These refer to non-specific people and things, in contrast to the definite articles, which refer to specific ones.

Just as we did with the der-words, the indefinite articles can be used in all of the forms. They simply change the endings based on the noun with which they are used. For example: "der Mann" (the man) becomes "ein Mann" (a man), but "die Frau" (the woman) becomes "eine Frau" (a woman).

You can't use "a" or "an" with a plural noun in English. The same is true in German. "A books" wouldn't make sense in either language. You can't use an indefinite article in front of a plural noun. You can, however, use other words that resemble indefinite articles in German. Most notably, the negative word "kein" (similar to "no" when used with a noun in English). This is the reason I put (k) on the chart in the plural form.

	Masculine	Feminine	Neuter	Plural
Nominative	ein	eine	ein	*(k)eine

When using the negative word "kein", you follow the exact same pattern. You would say "kein Mann" ("no man" or "not a man") and "keine Frau" ("no woman" or "not a woman"). When you get to the plural forms, you add -e to the end of "kein". For example: "keine Kinder" ("no children" or "not children")

In addition to "kein" there are possessive adjectives. Those are: mein (my), dein (your, singular, informal), sein (his or its), ihr (her or their) unser (our), euer (your, plural, informal) and Ihr (your, singular or plural, formal).

All of these words use the same last letters as the indefinite articles do. When combined with the indefinite articles, we call them "ein-words" for similar reasons to why we called the other ones "der-words". Below is the same chart that I used for the der-words, but for ein-words.

	Masculine	Feminine	Neuter	Plural
Nominative	ein	eine	ein	*(k)eine
Nominative	mein	meine	mein	meine

Let's take a look at a few example sentences using these "ein-words".

**Mein Hund ist mein bester Freund. -
My dog is my best friend.**

In this sentence we have "mein Hund" as the subject. We do not need an ending on "mein" in this sentence, as "Hund" is a masculine noun and when a masculine noun is the subject, you don't add any additional letters. That's just how the nominative case works.

You may also notice that "mein" is used for "mein bester Freund". You would rightly assume that the friend is both masculine and nominative in this sentence, as well. This is due to the special nature of the word "ist", but I explain that in a bit more detail later in this chapter. I just wanted to point it out here before we move on.

**Eine Katze ist in deinem Garten. -
A cat is in your garden.**

"Eine Katze" is the subject and therefore nominative. It is feminine and uses the indefinite article "eine" to indicate this.

The phrase "in meinem Garten" is a prepositional phrase. Basically, it is a tiny word, "in", followed by a noun "Garten" that is kind of attached to that little word. These types of phrases are used to describe locations among other supporting details in the sentence. There are quite a few of these in German and they are explained in more detail later in this book.

"Eine Katze" is the important part of this sentence, as it is the one doing something. Even though all it is "doing" in this sentence is "being", it is still the subject and nominative.

**Ein Schaf mäht. -
A sheep bleats (or mows?*).**

The verb "mähen" in German can mean "to bleat", as in the sound that sheep make. It can also mean "to mow". Context usually tells you which one is meant, but the only reason I used it is because I thought it was silly.

The important part in this sentence is that the noun "Schaf" (sheep) is the subject of the sentence, as it is the one making the noise. We use the article "ein" to indicate the neuter gender and the nominative case with this noun.

**Seine Haustiere sind zahm. -
His pets are tame.**

"Seine Haustiere" indicates that the pets are plural through the -e at the end of the possessive article "sein". This is also shown through the conjugation of the verb "sind", as this is the version that is used with the plural form "they" in German.

Complete workbook section 2.2 and 2.3 before continuing.

Nominative Personal Pronouns

There are a variety of types of pronouns I explain throughout the chapters of this book. The ones I have been using in example sentences have mostly been personal pronouns.

While these are the most common type of pronoun, there are also several other kinds of pronouns. I'll cover all of these topics in the coming chapters, but for this chapter we are going to focus on the personal pronouns.

Pronouns replace nouns. This means instead of saying the same object over and over again, we can replace the object with something shorter and easier to say. Instead of saying your own name in conversation, for example, you say "I" in English. Instead of "the man" you might say "he".

Think of pronouns as the nicknames of the German language. While there are tons of options to choose from for nicknames in real life, in German there are a select few that can be used and the have to be used in specific circumstances.

When you hear the word pronoun, you are likely already thinking of personal pronouns both in English and in German. They are the ones that are the most generic in their use and can replace pretty much any noun (person, place or thing) within a sentence. When in doubt, using the personal pronouns is the easiest and most likely option.

Personal pronouns are sometimes the same between nominative and accusative, but when we get to the dative case, everything is different from the nominative version. I'll mention in the genitive case chapter that the genitive case technically has pronouns, but they are looped in with the possessive articles, so it is best to think of them in their own category instead of keeping them in the same spot as the rest of the personal pronouns.

One thing to keep in mind with German pronouns is that the difference between "er", "sie" and "es" is more closely tied to the grammatical gender of the noun that the replace than the intrinsic gender of the person or animal to whom they refer.

This means you use the neuter pronoun to replace neuter nouns, even when they are "Schneewittchen" (Snow White), because -chen requires the neuter gender and the neuter pronoun is "es".

All of the personal pronouns in the nominative, accusative and dative cases are listed below.

Nom	Akk	Dat
ich	mich	mir
du	dich	dir
er	ihn	ihm
sie	sie	ihr
es	es	ihm

Nom	Akk	Dat
wir	uns	uns
ihr	euch	euch
sie	sie	ihnen
Sie	Sie	Ihnen

The nominative case pronouns are the ones you will see over and over again in the example sentences throughout this book. I have tried to limit my use of the other columns until we got to this chapter.

The nominative case pronouns are used to replace the subject of the sentence. They show us who or what is doing something within the sentence. If the person speaking is also the one doing the action in the sentence, they have two options, "ich" (I), if it is just them doing something or "wir" (we), if someone else is involved. These are called 1st person pronouns.

3rd person pronouns are "er" (he or masculine it), "sie" (she or feminine it) and "es" (neuter it) as well as the plural pronoun "sie" (they). These are used when the person to whom they refer is not in the conversation at all. The most difficult part about these pronouns is that you have to remember the gender that matters is the grammatical one, not the intrinsic one.

2nd person pronouns are the three "you's" in German; du, ihr and Sie. These are all used when speaking directly to the person mentioned in the sentence. They are also the most difficult to grasp, which is why I saved them for last.

The one that you need to know first is "Sie". This is the formal version. It can be used in the singular form (addressing one person) or in the plural form (addressing more than one person).

While I call this the "formal version", it isn't necessarily overly formal. What I mean by this is you don't have to use "Sie" just with suits and ties.

It is actually much more simple than that. For the most part, this form is used with people you don't know, but more specifically, it is used with people you don't know well.

For instance: You would definitely use "Sie" with the police officer who just pulled you over, but what about the cashier at the local grocery store? You go in there two or three times per week and you always go through their line. You know them, sort of, but you would still address them as "Sie". This form is used for your doctor, any cashier, waiter or waitress, public servant, or even a stranger on the street. Here a few examples of when you would use "Sie".

You are asking your teacher a question after class.

**Entschuldigen Sie. Können Sie mir helfen? -
Excuse me. Can you help me?**

You are asking for directions on the street.

**Können Sie mir sagen, wo der Hauptbahnhof ist? -
Can you tell me where the main train station is?**

You are at the checkout counter at Aldi and the cashier asks,

**Brauchen Sie heute eine Einkaufstasche? -
Do you need a shopping bag today?**

Your waiter comes to your table to get your order.

**Bringen Sie mir den Rinderbraten, bitte. -
Please bring me the roast beef.**

Since you are likely either just visiting Germany, most of the people you meet should be addressed with "Sie". This is because you aren't familiar enough with any of those people to use the other forms. This form is also easier for beginners to conjugate (that means your subject and your verb match forms). The present tense verb form is almost always the same as the infinitive (the version you will see when you look up a verb in the dictionary).

It might be easier to understand when to use "Sie", if you understand how to use "du" and "ihr". Both of these versions of "you" are informal. This is used with friends of yours and family members. It is also used with pets, children up to about the age of 15, students, fellow blue collar workers, and members of certain clubs.

The rule of thumb I use is, "Do I address this person as Mr., Mrs., or just by their first name?" or in short: If in doubt use Sie. If I use their first name, I probably use "du" with them. This isn't always true, however, as most waiters and waitresses will introduce themselves with their first name, but you will use "Sie" with them.

While "Sie" can be used to address one or more people, "du" can only be used to address one person at a time. If you are saying "you all", "y'all" or "you guys", you use "ihr". Here are a few examples:

Talking to your brother or your sister.

Was machst du heute? - What are you doing today?

Talking to your brother *and* your sister.

Was macht ihr heute? - What are you doing today?

Talking to your dog.

Du bist ein braver Hund. - You are a good dog.

Talking to your cats.

Ihr dürft nicht auf das Sofa. - You aren't allowed on the sofa.

Talking to your neighbor's four year old boy.

**Hast du ein neues Fahrrad? -
Do you have a new bicycle?**

That child responds to you.

**Ich habe dieses Fahrrad seit Mai.
Haben Sie es noch nicht gesehen? -
I have had this bicycle since may.
Have you not seen it?**

Talking to your neighbor's children.

**Habt ihr einen Hund zu Hause? -
Do you have a dog at home?**

The children answer your question with:

**Ja. Wollen Sie ihn treffen? -
Yes. Do you want to meet him?**

The only time that you have this uneven "du" and "Sie" conversation is when an adult is speaking with a child. The child uses the "Sie" form with the adult and the adult uses the "du" form when speaking to the child. In any other situation, the form of address will be the same for both speakers.

If you haven't picked up on the pattern yet, when you use "Sie" as the subject of your sentence, the verb ends with -en. "Ihr" requires -t and "du" requires -st. Getting the subject and verb to match or agree is called conjugation.

Let me show you a few examples side-by-side with each of the forms, so you can see this more clearly.

**Gehst du nach Hause?
Geht ihr nach Hause?
Gehen Sie nach Hause? -
Are you going home?**

Was kaufst du online?
Was kauft ihr online?
Was kaufen Sie online? -
What are you buying online?

Du kennst mich nicht.
Ihr kennt mich nicht.
Sie kennen mich nicht. -
You don't know me.

As a non-native speaker, I would recommend waiting for the German to offer the "du" form to you rather than offering in the opposite direction. Offering the "du" form to someone is always done from the older person or person of higher rank and not the other way around. This rule of thumb will help you avoid the awkward "Danke aber ich würde gerne beim Sie bleiben." (Thanks, but I would prefer to remain with "Sie".)

In order to offer the "du" form to someone, Germans use a variety of different phrases. The most common ones would include:

Sie können gerne "du" zu mir sagen.
Sie können mich ruhig duzen. -
You can say "du" to me.

Wir sagen "du" hier. -
We say "du" here.

Wollen wir uns nicht duzen? -
Don't we want to say "du" to each other?

You'll notice that even when offering the "du" form to someone, Germans will remain with the "Sie" form, as the person being offered the "du" form hasn't accepted yet. It is also common to avoid using "du" or "Sie" when offering the "du" form, as was shown in the last example.

Now that we know what the nominative case personal pronouns mean and how they are used, we can see them in example sentences.

Ich bin ein Mann. -
I am a man.

Bist du eine Lehrerin? -
Are you a teacher?

Der nette Mann ist hübsch. Er ist mein Sohn. -
The nice man is handsome. He is my son.

This example required me to use two sentences, as "er" requires us to first be aware of what or whom the pronoun is referring. "Er" refers back to "der nette Mann", which is why we used the masculine pronoun.

Die kluge Frau ist da drüben. Sie ist meine Tochter. -
The smart woman is over there. She is my daughter.

Following the same pattern, we used "sie" as a pronoun instead of saying "die kluge Frau" again. Sine "Frau" is a feminine noun, we use the feminine pronoun to replace her.

Das große Pferd ist braun. Es steht da. -
The large horse is brown. It stands there.

While this horse undoubtedly has an intrinsic gender, the word for horse (Pferd) is neuter, so we use the neuter pronoun, "es".

Wir fahren in die Stadt. -
We are driving into the city.

In this example we don't necessarily need to identify the people represented by the pronoun "we", as the person saying it is part of that group. It is simply the speaker plus one or more other people.

Bleibt ihr heute zu Hause? -
Are you staying at home today?

Das sind meine Kinder. Sie sind müde. -
These are my children. They are tired.

It may start out as a bit confusing that the pronouns "sie" shows up three different times in the nominative case pronouns list, but it is made easier through context. Since the verb "sein" is conjugated to the plural form "sind", we know "sie" in the second sentence either means "they" or "you". The first sentence took away any remaining ambiguity, as it shows us that "sie" refers back to the children in the first sentence. This means the only logical translation is "they".

Wie heißen Sie? -
How are you called?
(What is your name?)

This example shows us the formal you again. If you translate it literally, you end up with the first translation "How are you called?" This feels very unnatural in English, however, as we would rather say "What is your name?"

Complete workbook sections 2.4 - 2.7 before continuing.

Nominative Question Words

In case you didn't know, "question words" (i.e. who, what, when, where, why, etc. in English) are also known as "interrogative pronouns". Basically they are pronouns that ask questions. This means they replace things within sentences, specifically the information we want to know. Sometimes those question words require us to understand the German case system, so they are included in this book.

While there are a plethora of question words that are not affected by the case system, when we are asking questions about people and things (i.e. nouns), we do have to use the case system.

One of the very first question words that German learners encounter is the question word "wer". This is essentially the same as the English question word "who". Unfortunately for most native English speakers, we don't really understand the difference between "who" and "whom". This causes us to have some issues with understanding the difference between the various question words for people in German.

The question word "wer" can only be used to ask about a person who is the subject of the sentence. This means either you have a predicate noun in the sentence or there is no other subject to be seen in the sentence other than the question word.

Wer = Who
Wer ist das? - Who is that?
Das ist mein Mann. - That is my husband.

In this example, we have a whole lot of stuff written in red, because there are subjects and predicate nouns everywhere. In the question "Wer ist das?" the person "being" in that sentence is either "that" or "who", but due to the nature of the verb "sein", it is basically the same thing said twice.

We can see this illustrated more fully in the answer to the question "Das ist mein Mann." "Mein Mann" is technically the predicate noun of that sentence, but it definitely feels more like the subject. It says "mein Mann" instead of the accusative version "meinen Mann", because it is in the nominative case.

Wer lädt dich ein? - Who is inviting you?
Dein Mann lädt mich ein. - Your husband is inviting me.*

In this sentence we have a bit more variety. The one doing the inviting in the question and in the answer is in the nominative case. "Wer" is a kind of placeholder that shows us we lack some information. This is why we are asking a question about this information. The information that is missing here is "dein Mann". This is again shown in the nominative case, as he is the one doing the inviting.

A cool side effect of the question words for people is that it follows the last letter of the masculine articles. So, where we can use "wer", we can simply replace it with something that starts with "der". The last letter of the question word for people will match the case ending for masculine nouns.

Wer lädt dich ein? - Who is inviting you?
Der Mann lädt mich ein. - The man is inviting me.

I have to point out that the verb "einladen" generally carries with it the meaning that the person doing the inviting is paying for the activity, if there is some sort of price associated with it. For example:

Dein Mann lädt mich ins Kino ein. -
Your husband is inviting me to the movies.

Since your husband is the one doing the inviting, this sentence implies that your husband is paying for the tickets. It probably also implies that you are getting a divorce, but that is more of a social implication and not a grammatical or linguistic one.

In addition to the question word "wer", we can also ask about things (rather than people) in the nominative case using the question word "was" (what). While "wer" is always used with the nominative case, "was" can be used in either the nominative or the accusative cases.

Was = What

Was ist das? - What is that?

Here we see the exact same sentence that I used for the first "wer" example. We can ask this same question about things or people. Simply point to a thing and say "Was ist das?" or point to a person and ask "Wer ist das?"

The end result is the same. We are talking about something that is the subject, so we need the nominative case "was" to ask that question.

Was macht dieses Geräusch? -
What is making that sound?

You can also use it in more complicated sentences, although it is slightly more difficult to do so given the amount of times you need to use "what" as a subject, meaning it is doing something, but isn't a person.

Complete workbook section 2.8 before continuing.

Predicate Nouns

Now let's move on to the second use for the nominative case, predicate nouns. These are also called "predicate nominatives". If you are familiar with what a predicate is, you can already figure out what these things are.

The predicate is the part of the sentence after the verb. (Some definitions also include the verb in the definition of the predicate, but this does not change what we are talking about here.) Generally speaking, this is reserved for objects of the verb, which are used in cases other than nominative. When we say "nominative" we mean that it acts like the subject. That is why a "predicate nominative" is a restating of the subject after the verb.

To put it more simply, if you can put an equal sign where the verb is and the sentence still retains the same meaning, you are working with a predicate noun. You have already seen several examples of this in this chapter.

There are a select few verbs that can use these predicate nouns; sein (to be), werden (will, basically the future version of "sein") and bleiben (to remain or stay).

Ich bin ein Mann. -
I am a man.

In this sentence both "a man" and "I" are the subject of the sentence. It doesn't matter if the sentence says "Ich bin ein Mann." or "Ein Mann bin ich.", the end result is the same. You could put an equal sign where "bin" is and the meaning would be the same. "I = a man." All of this means that you have to use the nominative case on both sides of the verb "bin". Both "ich" and "ein Mann" indicate the nominative case.

Er wird mein fünfter Mann. -
He becomes (will be) my fifth husband.

Both "er" and "mein fünfter Mann" are written in the nominative case. That is because one is turning into the other. Again, our test works. If you put an equal sign where the verb "wird" is, the sentence still has pretty much the same meaning. "He = my 5th husband".

Sie bleibt meine Freundin. -
She remains my girlfriend.

She is not changing this time. In fact, she used to be my girlfriend and at the end of this sentence, she is still my girlfriend. If you put an equal sign where the verb "bleibt" is, you end up with the same meaning. "She = my girlfriend."

It is important to note that a predicate nominative is not a direct object. It is not being acted upon by the subject. "I" is not doing anything to "ein Mann" in the first example. "He" is not doing anything to "my fifth husband" in the second and so on. Each of these basically have an equal sign as a verb.

It is important to pay attention to this distinction, as this will make a big difference when we get to reflexive pronouns later on. This is when the subject and the object are the same person, but the subject is acting upon the object. Trust me, it will make sense when I explain those later.

For now, just know that, if you can't use an equal sign instead of the verb, you don't have a predicate nominative.

Complete workbook section 2.9 before continuing.

Directly Addressing People

The last time that we use the nominative case is when addressing people directly. Most of the time you won't have to care that this is nominative, but there are a few times that this will come in handy.

Junger Mann, tu das bitte nicht. -
Young man, please don't do that.

We are directly speaking to the young man in this sentence, which is why we used "junger" instead of "jung" with some other ending. The young man is not really a part of anything in the main sentence. He is simply being called out before the sentence continues.

Mein lieber Mann, ich will mich von dir scheiden lassen. - My dear husband, I want to get (myself) divorced from you.

"Mein lieber Mann" is in the nominative case here, which we can tell through the non-existent ending on "mein" and the -er at the end of the adjective "lieber". When we get to adjective endings later in this book, I'll explain the -er at the end, but for now, just understand that we are using the nominative case with "my dear husband", because we are addressing him directly.

This kind of use of the nominative case will come in handy if you ever write an email or a letter. The bottom line is that you use the nominative case when directly addressing someone. Most of the time this won't matter, but when it does matter, it is nice to know this kind of thing.

Nominative Case Review

To review, the nominative case is the baseline for all other cases. When you look up a word in a dictionary, the article (word for "the") you see in front of the noun is shown in the nominative case.

This case is mostly used for the subject of the sentence or even a restating of the subject after the verb (known as a predicate noun). You can also use the nominative case when directly addressing people. The definite articles (words for "the") in this case are "der" for masculine nouns, "die" for feminine nouns, "das" for neuter nouns and "die" for plural nouns.

In addition to all of this, there are two question words that rely on the nominative case to express their meaning. "Wer" is used to ask about people and is best translated with the English word "who". "Was" is used to ask about non-human things and is best translated with the English word "what".

If you haven't already, test your knowledge of the nominative case and all of the topics explained in this chapter by completing the worksheets in chapter 2 of the workbook or in the folder linked below.

https://www.germanwithantrim.com/mastering-cases/

Accusative Case

First, what is the accusative case? Generally, it is used for direct objects (don't worry if you don't know what that is, I'll explain in this chapter). There is a lot of overlap between the nominative case and the accusative case, which is why this is usually the second case that German learners encounter in a German class.

The accusative case is also used for a few other uses including: specific time and a variety of prepositions. I explain all of those things in this chapter.

Direct Objects

So what is a direct object? The nominative case is reserved for the subject of the sentence, the person or thing acting within the sentence. When the action completed by the subject is done in the direction of someone or something, that person or thing is usually shown in the accusative case.

The definition that first showed up when I googled "direct object definition" was:

> *a noun phrase denoting a person or thing*
> *that is the recipient of the action of a transitive verb*

This is a pretty awful definition. Do you have any idea what a "transitive verb" is? No. Great. You don't need to.

My definition is super simple.

The direct object is what is being verbed in the sentence!
- Herr Antrim

I understand that the word "verb" is not a verb, which means you can't "verb" things. But, if you are "verbing" something, that thing is the direct object. If I'm buying something, that something is the direct object. If I'm throwing something, that something is the direct object. If I like something, that something is the direct object.

So basically, whatever is being acted on in the sentence is the direct object. Let's try some examples.

38

Ich werfe den Ball. - I am throwing the ball.

"Den Ball" is the direct object. It is being thrown, which is why we used the article "den" to indicate the accusative masculine form for the noun.

Er mag dich. - He likes you.

"You" are the direct object here, which is why we used the accusative pronoun "dich" instead of the nominative pronoun "du". Pronouns are covered in more detail later in this chapter.

**Der Mann kauft den Traktor. -
The man is buying the tractor.**

"Der Mann" is the one buying something, which makes him the subject of the sentence and therefore nominative. The thing he is buying is the tractor, which gives us the accusative direct object of the sentence "den Traktor".

**Das Mädchen liest das Buch. -
The girl is reading the book.**

The girl is the subject, as she is the one reading something. This makes her use the nominative case. The book is the thing being read, which is why it uses the accusative case, as the direct object.

Definite Articles

In case you have forgotten, when I say "definite articles" I am referring to a category of words that basically translate as "the" in English. These usually are represented by "der", "die" and "das". They change, however, when the are not the nominative versions. You can see the change between the nominative and accusative cases in the chart on the next page.

	Masculine	Feminine	Neuter	Plural
Nominative	der	die	das	die
Accusative	den	die	das	die

As you can see, the only change is in the masculine form. The article changes from "der" to "den". This gives us the second line of our mnemonic device. Take the last letter of each word in the chart and combine them into a word for each line. RESE (ressa) NESE (nessa).

Of course these endings also apply to the additional der-words such as dieser, jeder and so on. The chart below includes them.

	Masculine	Feminine	Neuter	Plural
Nominative	der	die	das	die
Accusative	den	die	das	die
Nominative	dieser	diese	dieses	diese
Accusative	diesen	diese	dieses	diese

Again, the only change is for the masculine article. "Dieser" changes to "diesen". Don't forget that this is just an example and the last letter is really the only part that matters.

Here are a few more examples of direct objects. This time only using der-words.

**Der Mann hat den Ball. -
The man has the ball.**

"Der Mann" is the subject of the sentence in the nominative case, because he is the one that has something. The thing he has is "den Ball", which is the direct object and therefore displayed in the accusative case.

Die Frau bäckt/backt* die Torte. -
The woman bakes the cake.

The conjugation of "backen" is disputed. Some use an umlaut for the du and er, sie, es forms and others don't. That is the reason for my use of both in the example above.

The "Torte" is written in green here, as it is the thing being baked. This makes it the direct object and accusative. Don't forget that the article "die" does not change between nominative and accusative, so both "die Frau" and "die Torte" are written with the same article.

Das Mädchen sagt das Wort. -
The girl says the word.

"Das Mädchen" is the one saying something, which makes her the subject and nominative. The word is the thing she is saying, which gives us the direct object in the accusative case.

Die Kinder bauen die Sandburgen. -
The children build the sand castles.

The children are the subject of that sentence, as they are the ones building something. This makes them nominative. The something they are building are the sand castles, which are the direct object and in the accusative case.

Dieser Mann sieht jeden Film. -
This man sees every film.

"Dieser Mann" is the one seeing something, which makes him the subject and nominative. "Every film" is the direct object and accusative, as it is the thing being seen.

Diese Frau weiß jede Antwort. - This woman knows every answer.

"Diese Frau" is the one that knows something, which makes her the subject and nominative. "Every answer" is the direct object, which is why it is accusative.

Dieses Mädchen lässt dieses Buch zu Hause. - This girl leaves this book at home.

"This girl" is the subject who is leaving something, which is why she is in the nominative case. "This book" is the thing being left, which makes it the accusative case and the direct object. "Zu Hause" is a prepositional phrase using the dative case, which I will explain later in this chapter.

Diese Kinder finden alle Hinweise. - These children find all clues.

"These children" are the ones finding something and "all clues" are the things being found. This makes the children the subject and nominative and the clues the direct object in the accusative case.

Complete exercises 3.1 and 3.2 in the workbook before continuing.

Indefinite Articles

Just as with the definite articles, the only changes happen with masculine nouns. The masculine forms change from "ein" (no ending at all) to "einen" (-en added).

Just a quick reminder when you look at the charts on the next page: you will never use "eine" followed by a plural noun. Instead, this chart includes a kind of place holder to show that whatever additional ein-word you use has an -e at the end. Just remember that the possessive articles (mein, dein, sein, ihr, unser, euer, Ihr) and the negative article (kein) follow exactly the same endings in all of their forms.

	Masculine	Feminine	Neuter	Plural
Nominative	ein	eine	ein	(k)eine
Accusative	einen	eine	ein	(k)eine

	Masculine	Feminine	Neuter	Plural
Nominative	mein	meine	mein	meine
Accusative	meinen	meine	mein	meine

Here are a few example sentences using direct objects and indefinite articles.

**Ein Mann hält einen Hund in der Hand. -
A man is holding a dog in his hand.**

"Ein Mann" is the one holding something in this sentence, which makes him the subject in the nominative case. The dog is also masculine in this sentence, which is why we used the article "einen" in the accusative case.

**Eine Lehrerin unterrichtet eine Klasse. -
A teacher teaches a class.**

"Eine Lehrerin" is a female teacher, who is teaching a class. This makes her the subject of the sentence and nominative. "Eine Klasse" is also feminine, but it is the thing being taught, which is why it uses the accusative case. All of that is irrelevant, however, as the article is still "eine".

**Ein Mädchen führt ein Pony. -
A girl is leading a pony.**

"Ein Mädchen" is the one leading a pony, which uses the nominative case as the subject. "Ein Pony" is the thing being lead, which is the direct object and accusative.

Hopefully you get the idea, but I want to drive the point home with a few more examples. Follow the pattern I have shown you so far and try to identify why the red is red and the green is green in each of the following examples.

Meine Kinder bringen ihre Spielzeuge. -
My children bring their toys.

Sein Vater fragt unseren Kellner. -
His father asks our waiter.

Eure Mutter stellt ihre Frage. -
Your mother asks her question.

Unser Kind kennt mein sprechendes Pferd. -
Our child knows my talking horse.

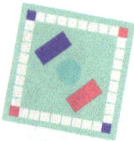

Ihre Kinder spielen meine Brettspiele. -
Their children play my board games.

Complete exercises 3.3 and 3.4 in the workbook before continuing.

Accusative Personal Pronouns

Almost any place you can use the accusative case, you can also use a pronoun. It could be the direct object or the object of one of the prepositions mentioned later in this chapter. No matter how it is being used, you still have the same main choices you had in the nominative case list.

There are still two 1st person pronouns, but instead of "ich" (I), you now say "mich" (me). Instead of "wir", you say "uns" in the accusative case.

There are still three 2nd person pronouns. "Du" changes to "dich". "Ihr" changes to "euch". The formal you does not change. It remains "Sie". The rules for these pronouns are the same as before.

The third person pronouns are mostly the same as before, but "er" changes to "ihn". These pronouns follow a pattern similar to the der-words. When "der" changes to "den", "er" changes to "ihn". "Sie" and "es" don't change in the accusative case in the same way that "das" and "die" are the same in both nominative and accusative. The plural "sie" is also the same, because "die" doesn't change in the plural form either.

Just as a reminder, this is what the chart for these pronouns looks like.

Nom	Akk	Dat
ich	mich	mir
du	dich	dir
er	ihn	ihm
sie	sie	ihr
es	es	ihm

Nom	Akk	Dat
wir	uns	uns
ihr	euch	euch
sie	sie	ihnen
Sie	Sie	Ihnen

Now let's see these pronouns in action.

Du brauchst mich. - You need me.

Ich brauche dich. - I need you.

I chose these two examples to show both the nominative and accusative forms of the top two pronouns. In the first example, you are the one that needs someone. That someone is "me", which is why we used the accusative version of "ich".

In the second example, "ich" is the one that needs someone. The someone I need is "you", which is represented by the accusative pronoun "dich".

Sie braucht ihn. - She needs him.

Er braucht sie. - He needs her.

Wir brauchen es. - We need it.

These three examples use the nominative and accusative forms of most of the 3rd person singular pronouns. The first two mirror each other, as one shows "she" needs someone and the other shows "he" needs someone. This changes our pronoun "er" into "ihn" for the first example. In English "she" changes to "her", but in German the pronoun "sie" does not change. The last example is just to round out the group and include a neuter example. "Es" remains "es" even when it is the direct object of the sentence.

Wir brauchen **euch**. - **We** need **you**.

Ihr braucht **uns**. - **You** need **us**.

In this mirrored pair we see "wir" changing to "uns" when used as the direct object and "ihr" changing to "euch". While "wir" mirrors the English change from "we" to "us", "ihr" does not mirror the English, as "you" remains "you" no matter how it is used within the sentence in English.

Sie brauchen **Sie**. - **They** need **you**.

Ich brauche **sie**. - **I** need **them**.

The last group shows another instance when the English pronoun changes and German does not. The accusative form of "sie" is still "sie", but in English "they" become "them" when used as the object (direct or indirect). Since "you" is always "you" in English, the lack of a change for "Sie" is not as confusing when comparing the two languages.

Complete exercises 3.5 - 3.7 in the workbook before continuing.

Accusative Question Words

When we are asking about a person in the accusative case, we need the German question word "wen". This indicates that the person is either the direct object of the sentence or the object of an accusative preposition. I've mentioned them several times now, so just be patient. They show up towards the end of this chapter.

Wer liebt **dich**? - **Who** loves **you**?
Wer lädt **dich** ein? - **Who** is inviting **you**?

vs

Wen liebst **du**? - **Whom** do **you** love?
Wen lädst **du** ein? - **Whom** are **you** inviting?

In the first two examples, the one who loves someone and the one who is inviting you are unknown and the subject of our question, so we use the question word "wer" (who). In the second set of questions we know the subject already, "du". This tells us that the person being loved and being invited is not the subject. They are the direct object. This means we have to use the question word "wen" to show the accusative case.

Luckily for both English speakers and German speakers there is a hint we can use to decide if we need "wer" or "wen" or even "who" or "whom". If you can answer the question with "er", you need "wer". The last letters match. If you can answer the question with "ihn", you need "wen". Again, note the last letters of each.

Wer lädt dich ein? - Who is inviting you?
Er lädt mich ein. - He is inviting me.

vs

Wen lädst du ein? - Whom are you inviting?
Ich lade ihn ein. - I am inviting him.

YOU'RE INVITED!

You can also use this logic in English. If you answer with "he", use "who". If you answer with "him", use "whom". While the last letters of the first question word doesn't match the answer, it does work for the second one. Conveniently, English only has one version of "him", so we don't have "whon" and "whom". If that were the case, this whole case problem in German would probably be a lot easier. Anyway, here is another example of the matching last letters game.

Wer liebt dich? - Who loves you?
Er liebt mich. - He loves me.
vs

Wen liebst du? - Whom do you love?
Ich liebe ihn. - I love him.

I mentioned before that you can use "was" in both the nominative and accusative cases. It is far more common to use it in the accusative case, as "was" refers to a non-person entity and those are more likely to be the object of the sentence rather than the subject. Here are a few examples to see what I mean.

Was ist das? - **What is that?**
Was frisst Hausaufgaben? - **What eats homework?**

vs

Was hast du in der Tasche? - **What do you have in the bag?**
Was isst du heute? - **What are you eating today?**

In the first set of examples, the question word is referring to a non-person as the subject, which means "was" is being used in the nominative case. Generally, no one cares that it is nominative, because it has no bearing on the sentence structure. I still believe it is important to notice, however, so you can answer with the nominative case. Instead of saying "den Hund" for the answer of the first one, you would use "der Hund", as we are asking about something nominative.

In the second set of examples we see "was" in the accusative case. It is asking about the direct object of each of those sentences. Again, I chose "du" as the subject, which is the one doing something and shown in the nominative case. The thing being "had" and "eaten" in these sentences are the direct objects and the question word "was".

Complete exercises 3.8 and 3.9 in the workbook before continuing.

Specific Time

The second use for the accusative case is "specific time". This, as the name implies, depicts a non-vague time. It isn't "some day" or "one day". It is "this day", "every day" or "this evening". Keep in mind that this is only used with the accusative case, if it is time expressed without a preposition. If there is a preposition, the case changes based on that preposition. Those will be explained at the end of this chapter.

Most of the time, it doesn't matter that the time is expressed with the accusative case. For example "heute Abend" or "heute Morgen". There are certain expressions, however, that use articles. That is when you need to pay attention to the fact that it is accusative.

Jeden Tag esse ich Wurst. -
Every day I eat sausage.

"Jeden Tag" is a specific time. It isn't just any day. It is every one of them. Because the time expression is not using a preposition in front of it and the noun "Tag" is masculine, we need the accusative masculine form "jeden" to go in front of "Tag".

**Jede Nacht schlafe ich sechs Stunden. -
Every night I sleep six hours.**

While the word "Nacht" is feminine, so we can't really tell if this phrase is nominative or accusative, we know it is accusative, because it is expressing a specific time. It can't be any of the other cases, as this would require an ending other than -e.

**Nächsten Dienstag spiele ich Fußball. -
Next Tuesday I am playing soccer.**

All days of the week are masculine in German. When used in the accusative case, we use -en at the end of the adjective. This is why "nächsten" ends with -en.

Complete exercise 3.10 in the workbook before continuing.

Accusative Prepositions

Prepositions are little words that you put in front of nouns or pronouns to give more context to the sentence at hand. While there are a bunch of different definitions for these words, this is the easiest way to think of them. Try not to overthink it. If a little word is directly in front of a noun or pronoun it is very likely a preposition.

Since nouns and pronouns require the case system when using the German language, we have to worry about the case that follows any particular prepositions.

There are a ton of prepositions in German, just like there are in English, but only a few use the accusative case. Technically there are eight, but some are more important than others.

The full list of accusative prepositions can be found below along with the song version. The song leaves out "wider", but you will be fine without that one, as I'll demonstrate later in this chapter.

If you sing the prepositions in the order listed below to the tune of "London Bridge is Falling Down", you can more easily remember which prepositions use the accusative case all of the time.

bis - until	♫ ♪
durch - through	**durch, für, gegen,** ♪
entlang - along	**ohne, um 3x** ♫
für - for	**durch, für, gegen** ♫
gegen - against	**ohne, um**
ohne - without	**bis und entlang**
um - around	**"London Bridge**
wider - contra	**is Falling Down"**

First on our list is "für". It looks and sounds a lot like the English preposition "for". It is often used in similar contexts, but not always. For example:

**Ich kaufe ein Geschenk für meine Mutter. -
I am buying a gift for my mother.**

**Er arbeitet für meinen Vater. -
He works for my father.**

These two examples show that you can do something "for someone" using the German preposition "für".

**Sie kauft diese Schuhe für dreißig Euro. -
She is buying these shoes for €30.**

If you are spending money on something, you can use "für" for that too.

**Karel möchte für immer jung sein. -
Karel wants to be young forever.**

You can even use "für" to describe a period of time, as you can see in this example.

50

If the word "das" is needed after "für", it is often shortened to "fürs". For example:

Ich kaufe die Karten fürs Konzert. - I am buying the tickets for the concert.

Meine Eltern geben zwanzig Euro fürs Fahrrad aus. - My parents are spending €20 for the bicycle.

The tricky part about using für isn't knowing what it means and how to use it. The problem is knowing when *not* to use it. There are a lot of occasions that English native speakers are tempted to use "für", because in English they would say "for". This is not always a good assumption.

You can use "für" when referring to time, but you more than likely mean to say something with the preposition "seit". If you want to use "für" followed by a period of time, you need to make sure that that time has concluded and is no longer continuing on. For example:

Ich habe für zwei Jahre bei einer Firma in der Stadt gearbeitet. - I worked at a company in the city for two years.

I'll give more examples of the preposition "seit" in the dative case chapter.

Wie viel Geld gibst du mir fürs (für das) Kaninchen? - How much money will you give me for the bunny?

Again you can see in this example, you can combine "für" and "das" in a contraction to form "fürs". These kinds of contractions are common in a lot ofdifferent prepositions, but I will show you each of them as they come up in the coming chapters.

If you are stating the purpose or reason for something, you don't use "für". Use "aus", "wegen" or "zu" instead. Those prepositions are covered in more detail in the dative and genitive chapters. "Aus" and "zu" use the dative case and "wegen" uses the genitive case.

Aus diesem Grund werden wir sie nicht einstellen. -
For this reason, we will not hire her.

Wegen der Erderwärmung sterben die Eisbären. -
Because of global warming, the polar bears are dying.

Dieses Haus ist nicht zum Verkauf. -
This house is not for sale.

If you are talking about a destination, use "nach" or "zu". When traveling to a city, state, country or like category of place, you need to use "nach", as you will see in the dative case chapter. If you mean that you are going to a place that could count as a building or inside of a city, use "zu".

Unser Flug fliegt um drei Uhr nach Berlin ab. -
Our flight departs for Berlin at 3 o'clock.

Wir fahren am Samstag zur Oma. -
We are headed for (driving to) grandma's on Saturday.

Next up on our list of accusative prepositions is "um". "Um" can best be translated with the English preposition "around". This will work most of the time. If you are going around something or one thing is around another, you likely need "um" in German. For example:

Der LKW fährt um das Auto. -
The semi truck drives around the car.

Die Fee streut einen Kreis aus Feenstaub um die Tiere. -
The fairy sprinkles a ring of fairy dust around the animals.

Der Koch wickelt das Kohlblatt um das Fleisch. -
The cook wraps the cabbage leaf around the meat.

Es geht rund ums (um das) Geld. -
It is all about money.

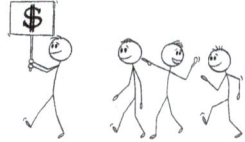

Similar to the way we contracted "für" and "das", you can also combine "um" and "das" to get "ums". You can see an example of that above.

You can also use "um" with a time of the day to say "at". For example:

Um zehn Uhr möchte ich essen. -
I would like to eat at ten o'clock.

Die Schule beginnt um acht Uhr. -
School begins at eight o'clock.

You may also see "um" followed by an infinitival clause, which includes the word "zu". This is used to say "in order to". For example:

Ich spare Geld, um ein Auto zu kaufen. -
I am saving money in order to buy a car.

When "um" is used in this way, it is not a preposition, but rather fulfilling the function of a conjunction, as it connects one clause to another. If you want to learn about how to make those clauses, I have a video on my YouTube channel about that, but conjunctions are not explicitly taught in this book.

Our next preposition is "durch". This is an easy one, as it is translated as "through" and is used pretty much the same as the English version. Here are a few examples:

Der Bus fährt durch den Tunnel. -
The bus drives through the tunnel.

Die Touristen gehen durch die Stadt. - **The tourists are walking through the city.**

Hänsel und Gretel laufen durch den Wald. - **Hansel and Gretel are walking through the forest.**

Danny fährt sein Dreirad durchs (durch das) Hotel. - **Danny rides his tricycle through the hotel.**

Another common contraction is "durch" plus "das" becoming "durchs". This one is a bit more difficult to say, which is why I don't personally use it much, but it does exist.

In addition to the literal meaning, you can use "durch" to mean something like "because of". For example:

Ich mache durch meine Erfahrungen auf YouTube bessere Videos. - **I make better videos because of (through) my experiences on YouTube.**

Mein Schreibtisch ist durch das Erdbeben kaputt gegangen. - **My desk was broken by the earthquake.**

Next on the list of accusative prepositions is "gegen". It is translated with the English word "against". For example:

Ich bin gegen Tierversuche. - **I am against animal experimentation.**

Der Junge schlägt seinen Kopf gegen die Wand. - **The boy hits his head against the wall.**

Was hast du gegen meinen Freund? -
What do you have against my friend?

Die Cardinals spielen morgen gegen die Cubs. -
The Cardinals are playing against the Cubs tomorrow.

Meine Mannschaft gewinnt gegen die Bösen. -
My team wins against the evil ones.

As you can probably guess, there are lots of examples when "gegen" could be substituted with "für" to mean you are for something instead of against it. You can fight for or against something. You can be for or against something. In those sentences, what you mean to say dictates which preposition you use.

"Gegen" can also be used to mean "against" an ailment or problem.

Ich nehme Aspirin gegen Kopfschmerzen. -
I take Aspirin for headaches.

You also use the preposition "gegen" with time. In this way it means "around".

Die Party beginnt gegen 7 Uhr. -
The party starts around 7 o'clock.

Der Klempner kommt gegen zehn Uhr. -
The plumber is coming around 10 o'clock.

The preposition "ohne" is translated with the English word "without". It is used almost exactly the same as that English preposition. That makes using "ohne" probably one of the easiest prepositions on the accusative list.

Ich kann ohne dich nicht leben. -
I can't live without you.

Pommes ohne Ketchup sind keine Pommes. -
Fries without ketchup are not fries.

Ich gehe nicht ohne einen Mantel aus dem Haus. -
I don't leave the house without a coat.

Ichabod sieht einen Mann ohne Kopf. -
Ichabod sees a man without a head.

Man lernt keine Grammatik ohne Beispiele. -
One doesn't learn grammar without examples.

The prepositions I have mentioned so far are usually the only ones listed in textbooks. That's because they are the most popular ones and the other ones sometimes require a bit more knowledge of the German language in order to use them properly. I'm going to talk about them anyway, starting with "bis".

The preposition "bis" generally means "until". You may recognize it from farewells, such as "bis später", "bis Morgen" or "bis Dienstag". Those all use the preposition "bis", but don't require us to remember that it's using the accusative case. When we use it with an article, however, we do have to remember that "bis" requires the accusative case. For example:

Bis nächste Woche! -
Until next week.

Bis nächsten Donnerstag. -
Until next Thursday.

56

"Bis" can also be translated with the English preposition "by", when it is expressing a deadline. For example:

Du musst **bis nächsten Dienstag deine Hausaufgaben** machen. - **You** have to do **your homework by next Tuesday**.

Bis nächstes Jahr werden **wir ein Haus** bauen. - **By next year we** will build **a house**.

"Bis" can't be used with an article, which is why it is often left off of lists like this, but it can be used with adjectives, which is what you saw in my examples. These will have the same endings as the definite articles in the accusative case. N for masculine, E for feminine and plural and S for neuter.

Another reason that "bis" is often left off of the accusative prepositions list is that it is often paired with another preposition, such as "zu" or "in". In those instances, "bis" is not in control of the case you use. You look to the other preposition to tell you the case.

Next on the list of neglected accusative prepositions in German, we have "wider". Not to be confused with "wieder", which sounds the same, but is definitely not the same. "Wider" means "against" or "contra", while "wieder" means "again". "Wider" is similar to "gegen", but sounds a bit out of date or elevated. For example:

Der Teenager rebelliert **wider den Vater**. - **The teenager** is rebelling **against the father**.

Dieser Film ist **wider meine Erwartungen**. - **This film** is **contra to my expectations**.

Man kann nicht **wider die Natur** agieren. - **One** cannot act **against nature**.

The last one on the accusative prepositions list is "entlang" and it comes with a bit of controversy. It is usually listed as an accusative preposition, but only uses the accusative case when it is in the postposition.

When "entlang" is used in front of a noun, it requires the genitive case. When it is used behind a noun, it uses the accusative case. Duden lists it as a preposition with the accusative case "bei Nachstellung" (with postposition) and even gives a few examples of how one might use it.

Unfortunately those examples are fragments of sentences and only show the noun and "entlang" after it. This doesn't tell me that it is a postposition. It shows me that the last word in the sentence is "entlang", which could just mean it is a separable prefix.

In fact, Duden also lists "entlang" as a separable prefix and as an adverb, so I know it can be done. You can see this when the infinitive of the verb is used at the end of the sentence and it is connected to the word "entlang". Such as: entlangfahren, entlangkommen, entlangführen, and many others.

Well, however you define this word, it can be translated with the English word "along", as in the following examples.

Wir fahren diese Straße entlang. -
We are driving along this street.

Wir fahren entlang dieser Straße. -
We are driving along this street.

In the second example I used the genitive case, because I put "entlang" in front of the noun.

Ich laufe entlang des Weges. -
I am walking along the path.

Ich laufe den Strand entlang. -
I am walking along the beach.

58

For these examples I started with the genitive one with the preposition directly before "des Weges". We took "der Weg" and changed it into the genitive case due to the preposition. In the second example, we used the accusative case, because "entlang" is after the noun.

Also keep in mind that masculine nouns require an -n at the end of whatever article or adjective you use in front of it when in the accusative case. The accusative pronouns will also be needed, if you have an accusative preposition.

You can now complete exercises 3.11 - 3.13 in the workbook.

Accusative Case Review

To review, the accusative case is primarily used to show what is being acted upon within the sentence. If something is being "verbed", that something is accusative.

The accusative case is also used for specific expressions of time. You can see the accusative case through the changing of masculine articles from "der" to "den" or "ein" to "einen". For all of the other genders and the plural nouns, the articles are the same as the nominative case.

In addition to all of that, there are a variety of prepositions that require the accusative case. As long as you remember the main five (für, um, durch, ohne and gegen) and you will be fine. The other accusative prepositions are a bit more rare or it really doesn't matter that they use the accusative case.

I'm sure you get the pattern by now, but this is the part where you practice what you have learned here. Complete the exercises in chapter 3 of the workbook or via the link below.

Extra materials for this chapter:
https://www.germanwithantrim.com/mastering-cases/

Dative Case

The dative case is primarily used with indirect objects. If you don't know what that is, don't worry, I'll explain shortly. In addition to indirect objects, the dative case is also used with dative verbs, certain dative phrases and certain prepositions.

There is almost no overlap between the nominative and accusative cases and the dative case when it comes to articles and pronouns. While the feminine, neuter and plural articles don't change between the nominative and accusative cases, everything changes in the dative case.

Indirect Objects

Since the main use of the dative case is indirect objects, let's start there. In the last chapter I explained what a direct object is. It is essentially the thing that is being acted upon by the subject. This was succinctly stated as "what is being verbed" in my definition. The indirect object is the recipient of that direct object.

Basically when the direct object is given, sent or otherwise pushed in the direction of a person or thing, that person or thing is an indirect object. Short version: who or what (usually a who) is receiving the direct object.

If you "verb" something in the direction of someone or something, you are using that person or thing in the indirect object spot within the sentence, which in German we indicate through the use of the dative case.

Ich gebe dem Mann den Kaffee. -
I am giving the man the coffee.

In this sentence, I am the one giving something. This makes "ich" the subject, which is why it is a nominative case pronoun. The thing that is being given within this sentence is "den Kaffee", which we can see through the masculine accusative case article "den". The person receiving the coffee in this sentence is "dem Mann". This is the indirect object and is shown in the dative case with the masculine article "dem".

It should also be noted that some German phrases still use the "dative -e", which makes it "dem Manne", as in "dem Manne kann geholfen werden" (the man can be helped).

60

Er kauft seiner Mutter eine Blume. -
He is buying his mother a flower.

The person doing something in this sentence is "er", which is in the nominative case. He is buying something. The something he is buying is "eine Blume", the direct object in the accusative case. The person receiving the flower in this sentence is "seiner Mutter". This makes her the indirect object of the sentence, which we indicate through the dative case. The feminine dative articles all end with -r. This is true for both definite and indefinite articles.

Wir schenken den Kindern Fahrräder. -
We are giving the children bicycles (as gifts).

The subject here is "wir", which is in the nominative case. The bicycles are the direct objects, which is why they are in the accusative case. The indirect object is "den Kindern", as the children are receiving the bicycles. This is why the article "den" is used to indicate the plural dative form and there is even an extra -n added to the plural form of the noun "Kind". Normally, the plural form is "Kinder", but the dative case requires an -n at the end of the noun, as well.

Definite Articles

Below is a chart for the definite articles. This time it includes the nominative, accusative and dative cases.

	Masculine	Feminine	Neuter	Plural
Nominative	der	die	das	die
Accusative	den	die	das	die
Dative	dem	der	dem	den (n)

RESE NESE MRMN

If you continue the mnemonic device pattern that we have used so far and look at the last letter of each word, you end up with the first three cases as: RESE (ressa), NESE (nessa), MRMN (Mr. Mann or Merman).

One irritating little bit about the dative case is that we now have our first instance of overlap between the articles of the cases that don't match the genders with which they were used before. The feminine article is now "der", which looks just like the masculine form from the nominative case. The plural article is now "den", which looks just like the masculine form from the accusative case. It is important not to get hung up on these kinds of oddities. You will be much better off, if you just look at it as "use this article in this situation and that article in the other situation".

	Masculine	Neuter	Feminine	Plural
Nominative	der	das	die	die
Accusative	den	das	die	die
Dative	dem	dem	der	den (n)

Some teachers and learners prefer to use this version of the chart, as it puts the similar articles next to each other. All four of the "die" articles are in the top right corner for feminine and plural while the two "dem" articles are together in the bottom left for the masculine and neuter forms in the dative case. This will work even better when the genitive case shows us more similarities between masculine and neuter.

I don't have a preference for either of the charts. I was taught with the first one, which is why I default to it, but I think learners should use whichever one makes the most sense to their brain.

	Masculine	Feminine	Neuter	Plural
Dative	dem	der	dem	den (n)
Dative	diesem	dieser	diesem	diesen (n)

This version of the chart includes an example of the additional der-words. Again, the important part is that the end of the words end with the letters from our mnemonic devices: RESE, NESE, MRMN.

You will notice from the dative plural form that in addition to the article ending with an -n there is an extra -n in parentheses. This is there to indicate that the noun will also use an -n at the end of it, unless, of course, if the plural form of the noun already ends with an -n. You also saw this in the example I gave earlier with the noun "Kinder", which in the dative case becomes "Kindern".

Singular - Plural - Plural Dative
das Kind - die Kinder - den Kindern
the child - the children - the children

Please note that nouns with -s added for the plural form will not add -n for the plural dative form. For example: "die Kulis" (the pens) in nominative just becomes "den Kulis" (the pens) in the dative case.

Der Arzt gibt dem Patienten den Zettel. -
The doctor gives the patient the slip of paper.

The patient is receiving the slip of paper, which is why we use the dative masculine article "dem". In a sneaky bit of foreshadowing, I threw in the word "Patient", which requires an -en when it is not the subject (or in the nominative case). This is an example of a weak noun, which shows up in a future chapter.

Die Schülerin sagt der Lehrerin die Antwort. -
The student tells the teacher the answer.

In this sentence the teacher is the recipient of the answer said by the student. This shows us the indirect object is the teacher, which requires the dative case. The feminine article in the dative case is "der".

Das Mädchen gibt dem Pferd das Heu. -
The girl gives the horse the hay. .

The horse is receiving the hay from the girl. That makes the horse the indirect object and in the dative case. The dative neuter article is "dem".

Die Eltern zeigen den Kindern die Spielzeuge. -
The parents show the children the toys.

In this example the children are the indirect object and in the dative case, because the toys are being shown in the direction of the children.

The dative plural article is "den" and the noun "Kinder" requires an extra -n at the end in the dative case.

Complete exercise 4.1 in the workbook before continuing.

Indefinite Articles

When we get to the indefinite articles in the dative case, the definite article endings finally match the indefinite article endings. The definite articles end with MRMN. The indefinite articles follow the exact same pattern. This is shown in the chart below.

	Masculine	Feminine	Neuter	Plural
Nominative	ein	eine	ein	(k)eine
Accusative	einen	eine	ein	(k)eine
Dative	einem	einer	einem	(k)einen (n)

Don't forget you can also use these same endings with the possessive articles (mein, dein, sein, ihr, unser, euer, Ihr) and the negative article (kein). You can see an example of that with the possessive article "mein" in the chart below.

	Masculine	Feminine	Neuter	Plural
Nominative	mein	meine	mein	meine
Accusative	meinen	meine	mein	meine
Dative	meinem	meiner	meinem	meinen (n)

Ein Junge bringt meinem Sohn einen Lutscher. - A boy brings my son a lollipop.

"Ein Junge" is the subject, "einen Lutscher" is the direct object and "meinem Sohn" is the indirect object. This means "a boy" is in the nominative case, "a lollipop" is in the accusative case and "my son" is in the dative case.

Eine Frau stellt ihrer Professorin eine Frage. - A woman asks her professor a question.

The professor in this sentence is receiving the question, which makes her the indirect object and therefore dative. The dative ending has to be -er, which is why "ihr" gets -er added to the end in this sentence.

Ein Mädchen erzählt ihrem Hampelmännchen ein Märchen. - A girl tells her jumping jack toy a fairytale.

The indirect object here is "ihrem Hampelmännchen", which is a neuter noun. This toy is receiving the direct object "Märchen" from the subject "ein Mädchen".

Meine Lehrer bringen meinen Mitschülern ihre Kenntnisse bei. - My teachers teach my classmates their knowledge.

In this sentence "my teachers" are the subject and nominative, while "ihre Kenntnisse" are the things being taught as the direct object and accusative. The last thing is "meinen Mitschülern", which includes an -n at the end of the possessive article "meinen" as well as the extra -n added to the usual plural form of "Mitschüler".

Complete exercise 4.2 in the workbook before continuing.

Dative Personal Pronouns

You can use dative pronouns whenever the dative case comes up, just like with accusative pronouns. This means, if you are using an indirect object, a dative verb, a dative phrase or one of the dative prepositions or two-way prepositions, you can use a dative pronoun.

Again, the third person singular and plural forms follow the pattern for der-word endings. This means when you use "dem" in front of a noun, you would use "ihm" as the pronoun. If you use "der" in the dative case for a feminine noun, the pronoun is "ihr". If you use "den" for the plural dative article, use "ihnen" for the pronoun.

As I have done the last two times I brought up personal pronouns, here is the personal pronoun chart for the first three cases.

Nom	Akk	Dat
ich	mich	mir
du	dich	dir
er	ihn	ihm
sie	sie	ihr
es	es	ihm

Nom	Akk	Dat
wir	uns	uns
ihr	euch	euch
sie	sie	ihnen
Sie	Sie	Ihnen

Let's look at some examples to see how you can use these in context and what the relationship is between the article endings and the personal pronoun endings.

Der Arzt gibt dem Patienten den Zettel. -
The doctor gives the patient the slip of paper.

Er gibt ihm den Zettel. -
He gives him the slip of paper.

In these examples we can clearly see a direct and indirect object. The doctor is the subject and is the one giving something. That makes him use the nominative case. The thing being given is the piece of paper, which is also masculine. This makes us use the accusative article "den". The one receiving the paper is the indirect object, "dem Patienten", which is shown in the dative case.

When we switch out "dem Patienten" with a pronoun, we use a pronoun that ends with the same letter as the article. Since "dem" ends with -m, we use "ihm" to replace "dem Patienten", as this pronoun also ends with -m.

While some would likely call this a happy little linguistic accident, I would like to think it was done to give German learners one small reprieve from the constant case system bombardment.

Die Schülerin sagt der Lehrerin die Antwort. -
The student tells the teacher the answer.

Die Schülerin sagt ihr die Antwort. -
The student tells her the answer.

66

This example follows a similar pattern. The first thing in the sentence is the subject, "die Schülerin", shown in the nominative case, as it is the subject. The thing being said is the direct object in the accusative case "die Antwort". The dative object is the indirect object "der Lehrerin".

Since the article "der" ends with -r, we know that our pronoun should also end with -r. The only option is "ihr".

Mein Opa gibt mir jedes Jahr 100€ zum Geburtstag. - My grandpa gives me €100 every year for my birthday.

When we aren't using the 3rd person pronouns, we simply have to remember the pronouns for their individual meanings to use them properly. The person saying this sentence is the same as the one receiving the €100, which is why we used the dative pronoun "mir" to say "me".

Deine Schwester kann dir bei den Hausaufgaben helfen. - Your sister can help you with the homework.

In this sentence we needed the 2nd person singular pronoun in the dative case, "dir". This shows that the person getting helped in this sentence is being directly spoken to and is in the dative case.

Das Restaurant serviert uns das Abendessen. - The restaurant is serving us dinner.

In this sentence we need to say that the speaker plus one or more other people are receiving the direct object. This makes the only appropriate pronoun "uns", which is German for "us".

Ich kaufe euch die Karten fürs Konzert. - I am buying you the tickets for the concert.

Here we see the plural informal version of "you" in the dative case as the receiver of the tickets .This means our pronoun in the dative case is "euch".

Das Mädchen gibt dem Pferd das Heu. -
The girl gives the horse the hay.

Das Mädchen gibt es ihm. -
The girl gives it it.

Here we used the same pattern. The girl is the subject, shown in the nominative case at the beginning of the sentence. The thing being given is the accusative direct object, "das Heu". The one receiving this direct object is the indirect object, "dem Pferd", shown in the dative case.

Just as we did in the previous examples, the pronouns' last letters match the last letters of the articles in front of the nouns they replace. "Das Heu" is replaced by "es" and "dem Pferd" is replaced by "ihm".

You may have noticed, however, that the word order changed. That is because of a weird quirk of the German sentence structure format. Basically, if the direct object is a pronoun, it goes before the indirect object.

Die Eltern zeigen den Kindern die Spielzeuge. -
The parents show the children the toys.

Die Eltern zeigen sie ihnen. -
The parents show them them.

You can see the same thing occur in this example. "Den Kindern" is replaced by the plural dative pronoun "ihnen" and "die Spielzeuge" is replaced by the plural accusative pronoun "sie". Because the direct object is a pronoun, it now shows up before the indirect object.

When you have both a direct and indirect object, you have two scenarios in which the indirect object would be first and two in which the direct object would be first.

If neither of those objects are pronouns, the indirect object goes first. If only the indirect object is a pronoun, the indirect object is still first. If only the direct object is a pronoun, the direct object goes first. If both the direct and indirect objects are pronouns, the direct object goes first.

You can see these scenarios mapped out in the illustration on the next page. Remember, "DO" stands for direct object, and "IO" stands for indirect object.

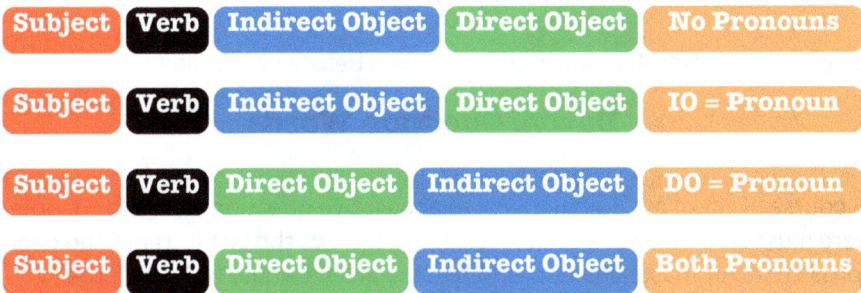

Subject	Verb	Indirect Object	Direct Object	No Pronouns
Subject	Verb	Indirect Object	Direct Object	IO = Pronoun
Subject	Verb	Direct Object	Indirect Object	DO = Pronoun
Subject	Verb	Direct Object	Indirect Object	Both Pronouns

If you don't want to think of it in terms of four scenarios, you can really boil it down to just two. Is the direct object a pronoun or not? If it is not, the indirect object goes first. If the direct object is a pronoun, the direct object goes first. The graphic below illustrates this with four versions of the exact same sentence.

Direct Object is NOT a Pronoun	Die Eltern zeigen den Kindern die Spielzeuge. - The parents show the children the toys. Die Eltern zeigen ihnen die Spielzeuge. - The parents show them the toys.
Direct Object IS a Pronoun	Die Eltern zeigen sie den Kindern. - The parents show the children them. Die Eltern zeigen sie ihnen. - The parents show them them.

After a lot of exposure to these kinds of sentences it will eventually become natural to switch the word order when the direct object is a pronoun. It just takes some practice. It really does roll off of the tongue more easily once you get used to it.

When working with personal pronouns, there are three categories to worry about. 1st person refers to either "ich" (I) or "wir" (we). This is where the speaker is the one speaking. 2nd person refers to "du" (you, singular, informal), "ihr" (you, plural, informal) and "Sie" (you, singular or plural, formal). 3rd person refers to "er" (he), "sie" (she), "es" (it) and "sie" (they).

These pronouns are the base forms and help us categorize the other pronouns in the accusative and dative cases. The same rules for the cases apply for the pronouns, but instead of worrying about articles and the like, we are only concerned with how the pronoun is being used in the sentence.

Complete exercises 4.3 - 4.6 in the workbook before continuing.

Dative Question Words

Of course, if there are nominative and accusative question words for people, there must also be a dative one. This again, follows the last letter of the der-words chart for masculine nouns. While the article would be "dem", the question word is "wem". In English we translate this word with "whom" just as we did for "wen". The difference is that this question word must be the indirect object, object of a dative verb or the object of a dative preposition.

Wem kaufst du es? -
(For) Whom are you buying it?

Here we see "wem" used as the indirect object of the sentence. The subject is "du", as "you" are buying something. The something being purchased is "es", which is the direct object in the accusative case. The person for whom the "it" is being purchased is not known, which is why we have to use the question word "wem" to inquire about it.

Wem schreibst du einen Brief? -
Whom are you writing a letter?

Just to be sure you understand how this works, here is another example using "wem" as the indirect object in the dative case. If you were relying on the word order before to tell you which case should be used, that trick does not work with question words unless you rearrange the question into a statement, as I showed you with "wer" and "wem". In sentences like these the question word "wem" has to be replaceable with the pronoun "ihm" in order for you to verify that "wem" is needed.

Wem hilfst du? -
Whom are you helping?

This sentence uses the verb "helfen", which requires a dative object. When we use a question word with this verb, we need to say "wem" to keep the dative case visible. The next section of this chapter explains dative verbs like "helfen" in more detail.

Mit wem arbeitest du? -
With whom do you work?

Here is an example of the dative preposition "mit", which requires the question word "wem" after it to show the dative case. This will happen with any of the dative prepositions. These are explained in more detail later in this chapter.

Complete exercise 4.7 in the workbook before continuing.

Dative Verbs

Dative verbs, as the name implies, are verbs that require a dative object. Specifically, they use the dative case with the direct object rather than the accusative case. This is generally applied to people, but it can be other things as well. This idea is best explained through examples.

Mein Bruder hilft unseren Eltern
mit der Hausreinigung. -
My brother helps our parents
with the housekeeping.

In this example "our parents" are the direct object, but instead of "unsere Eltern", which would indicate either the nominative or the accusative case, we used "unseren Eltern", which shows us the dative case is used. The reason is the verb "helfen". The object after "helfen", a dative verb, is dative.

You could think of it as the verb "helfen" absorbing the thing being given (the direct object). If you rephrase this sentence, you can see what I mean.

Mein Bruder gibt unseren Eltern
Hilfe mit der Hausreinigung. -
My brother gives our parents help
with the housekeeping.

In this version "my brother" is giving "help" as the direct object and the recipients of this help are "our parents". This makes them the indirect object, which is indicated with the dative case. While this is a bit of a stretch of logic, this is kind of why the verb "helfen" (and several other dative verbs) requires the dative case with the object.

Das T-Shirt passt dem Mann nicht. -
The t-shirt does not fit the man.

In this example we have "das T-Shirt" as our subject in the nominative case. The man is the direct object, but because it is the object of the dative verb "passen", we have to use the dative case instead of the accusative. The man is the person "to whom" the shirt does not fit.

This is another pattern that happens with lots of dative verbs. We say "to whom" in some translations, which shows us that the object is not the direct object, but instead a dative object that falls outside of the normal rules.

Die Fliege steht dir gut. -
The bow tie looks good on you.

The bow tie is the thing that looks good. This action of looking good is done for the benefit of "you" in this sentence, which is why we used the dative pronoun "dir". (Pronouns are explained in more detail later in this book.) This illustrates another pattern that comes up sometimes with dative verbs, which is that they are done "for the benefit" of some person. This causes the use of the dative case.

Diese Filme gefallen mir nicht. -
I do not like these films.
(Literally: These films are not pleasing to me.)

The verb "gefallen" is irritating to lots of German learners. It functions similarly to the Spanish verb "gustar", which basically takes English sentences about liking things, and flips them on their heads. The same is done with the verb "gefallen".

The subject of the sentence is the thing that is liked. The object is the person that likes it. It could more literally be translated as "These films are not pleasing to me." This again shows that it isn't a normal direct object, but rather a dative object of a dative verb.

**Der Kunde dankt dem Kellner. -
The customer thanks the waiter.**

The customer is the one doing something. The person receiving the thanks is the waiter, which shows a kind of absorbed direct object "thanks" and the indirect object object is the waiter. The dative case is shown through that object.

**Der Klasse fehlt Klaus heute. -
The class is missing Klaus today.**

The class is in the dative case here, because Klaus is the thing that is missing. You can think of it as "Klaus is missing to the class." It isn't like Klaus just disappeared or was kidnapped. He is only missing in connection to the class. He is missing "to the class". The rest of the world is still enjoying itself with Klaus intact.

So far you have seen examples of the dative verbs "helfen" (to help), "passen" (to fit), "stehen" (to look * on someone), "gefallen" (to like), "danken" (to thank) and "fehlen" (to be missing). These are some of the most common dative verbs, but there are about 50 of them in the entire German language.

At the end of the book there is a kind of quick reference grammar guide. In that guide you will find a huge list of these verbs. Until you get to that point, however, you should concentrate on the verbs that are listed on the next page, as they are the most commonly used dative verbs in the German language.

Once you get the hang of the common ones you can work your way towards the rest of the list.

On the next page you will find a list of the most common dative verbs you are most likely to encounter in German.

German	English	German	English
antworten	to answer (a person)	beantworten*	to answer (a question)
danken	to thank	gefallen	to please
gehören	to belong (to)	glauben	to believe
gratulieren	to congratulate	helfen	to help
passieren	to happen	schmecken	to taste

Just a heads up: The verb "antworten" has a counterpart that uses an accusative object instead of a dative one. While the verb "antworten" always uses a person as its object in the dative case, the verb "beantworten" uses a question as the direct object, which is always shown in the accusative case.

There are rare occasions when a dative verb can be used with an accusative object instead of the usual dative one. This is usually done when the verb is used with an object that is not a person. For example:

Ich glaube dir nicht. -
I don't believe you.

Ich glaube dir deine Geschichte nicht. -
I don't believe your story from you.

Ich glaube deine Geschichte nicht. -
I don't believe your story.

"You" in the first sentence is the dative object. You can add extra information to this sentence to make it use a direct object, which is what you see in the second example.

In the second example, we have a direct object "deine Geschichte", which tells us that it isn't the entire person that we don't believe, but rather the story that they are telling. We still used the dative object "dir" just like we did in the previous version, but now it is an indirect object, which is just normal dative case behavior.

You can remove the indirect object, as you see in the last example, and end up with a sentence that only has an accusative object.

This shows a very rare use of the verb "glauben", so it is important to remember that it usually requires a dative object.

Er verzeiht mir nicht. -
He doesn't forgive me.

Er verzeiht mir meinen Fehler nicht. -
He doesn't forgive me my mistake.

Er verzeiht meinen Fehler nicht. -
He does not forgive my mistake.

He is the one forgiving, which makes him nominative. The person being forgiven is the dative object "me". This is another example of a kind of "implied direct object", which is why you can also phrase this with the second and third examples.

In the second example, "the mistake" is direct object, which is why we used "meinen Fehler" in this sentence. It is the thing being forgiven. It is directly acted upon by the subject, which is why it uses the accusative case. The person in this sentence for whom the forgiveness is done, is "mir".

You could, of course, eliminate the dative pronoun "mir", which is what I did in the last example.

There are also certain verb prefixes that often indicate a dative verb. For example:

Er konnte seinem Schicksal nicht entgehen. -
He couldn't avoid his fate.

The inseparable prefix "ent-" is often attached to dative verbs. It has a general meaning of removing something, but most often is translated with the prefixes un-, de- or dis- in English. It can also carry with it the meaning of removing something.

Marlin schwimmt dem Doktorfisch nach. -
Marlin swims after the tang (fish).

When "nach" is used as a preposition, it requires the dative case. When it is used as a separable prefix, it is also used with the dative case.

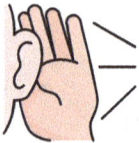

**Hört mir zu! -
Listen to me.**

The preposition "zu" is also used with the dative case. Again, when it becomes a separable prefix, it uses the dative case.

Complete exercises 4.8 - 4.11 before continuing.

Special Dative Phrases

There are also several special dative constructions or special dative phrases that require the dative case. This is most commonly used with the verb "sein" and certain adjectives. The fact that it uses the verb "sein" makes some people think that the dative case is used with the verb "sein", but it is actually the adjective that creates the need for the dative case. It is called "the dative of interest".

**Es ist mir kalt/kühl/warm/heiß. -
It is cold/cool/warm/hot to me.**

**Mir ist kalt/kühl/warm/heiß. -
It is cold/cool/warm/hot to me.**

The most common way this is used is with temperatures. The original version of this phrasing is shown on the first line above. While this version has "es" in the sentence to say "it is...", the more modern version has lost the word "es" and become the second example.

If you are describing the temperature around a person, you use this kind of phrasing to do it. If you made the mistake of saying "Ich bin kalt.", you are essentially saying you are emotionally aloof or actually physically cold, which means you are dead or suffering from hypothermia. The other temperatures also have their own weird translations, if you don't use the dative construction. Just make sure you don't make those mistakes.

You can see this in the examples below using the third person pronouns "er" (he) and "ihm" (him). If "he" is nominative, we are talking about his emotions or physical state. If "he" is dative, we are talking about his perception of the temperature around him.

Ihm ist kalt. - **He is cold.** (**It is cold to him.**)
Er ist kalt. - **He is cold.** (**He shows little emotion.**)

Lots of these dative constructions will not use a subject, which makes them look pretty weird. This is usually because there is a sort of implied "es" like we had in the previous example. You could simply say, "Es ist kalt." (It is cold.) and avoid the dative part entirely.

When you want to talk about the temperature in relation to a person, you need to use the dative case. Instead of using a phrase like "Es ist mir kalt.", we use "Mir ist kalt." to shorten the sentence and make it simpler.

Er ist seinem Vater sehr ähnlich. -
He is very similar to his father.

This means that he is similar in relation to his father. Instead of using a prepositional phrase like the English phrase did, we use the dative case to kind of side step that.

Ich bin diesem Mann dankbar. -
I am thankful to this man.

Again, the thankfulness is directed at a person, which is used in the dative case. This is done with a preposition (to) in English, but a dative object in German.

Es kommt mir fremd vor. -
That seems foreign to me.

This is exactly the same pattern. The English preposition "to" makes another appearance, while the German version simply uses the dative case.

The following adjectives use similar constructions with the dative case in German.

ähnlich	angenehm	begreiflich	behilflich
(un)bekannt	bequem	dankbar	fremd
gleich	leicht	nützlich	peinlich
richtig	schädlich	teuer	überlegen
verwandt	wichtig	willkommen	

The bottom line for these kinds of phrases is to ask yourself, "Is this literally describing the subject or the relationship to the subject?" If an adjective from this list is describing the subject, there is no need for the dative case. If it is describing the relationship between the subject and some other object, that other object should be shown in the dative case.

Complete exercises 4.12 and 4.13 in the workbook before continuing.

Dative Prepositions

Just as there are accusative prepositions, there are some prepositions that always use the dative case. There are nine of them. You can see them listed below along with their song version. Unfortunately, the song leaves off one of the prepositions, again. Some teachers simply tack it on to the end of the song in the most tacky way possible (pun intended), while others (like me) simply remind their students that "gegenüber" exists and it requires the dative case.

If you sing the prepositions on the list below to the tune of "The Danube Waltz", you will more easily remember which prepositions always use the dative case. If you don't know "The Danube Waltz", you probably actually do. Google it. Give it a listen and then it will make sense. Alternatively, there is a video of me singing all of the prepositions songs on YouTube. Just search for "German prepositions songs" and look for the bow tie.

aus - out of, from
außer - except, besides, in addition to
bei - at, with, near, by
mit - with
nach - after, to, towards
seit - since, for (time)
von - from
zu - to, at (home)
gegenüber - across from

♫ An der schönen, ♪ ♫ ♪ blauen Donau, The Danube Waltz

"aus" means out of or from. It is used to show that something was in something and is now no longer. This is different from "von", which is also on our list for today and will be explained in more detail in a bit. For now, I'll show you a few examples of how to use "aus".

Ich komme aus den USA. -
I am from the USA.
(I come from the USA.)

I was once in the USA. That is my place of origin. Now I am expressing that I came out of that place with the preposition "aus". And you cannot say this while being in the US, because then you would say "Ich bin von hier.", as you are still currently there. No exiting has occurred.

Meine Oma holt mir Schokolade aus der Schublade. -
My grandma gets me chocolate from the drawer.

Wir fahren heute aus der Stadt. -
We are driving out of town today.

Wann kommst du aus der Schule? -
When do you get out of school?

Aus frischem Käse macht man den besten Käsetoast. -
From fresh cheese, one makes the best grilled cheese.

In the last example we get the other use of the translation "out of". This means something like "from these parts". It is used in the same way in both languages.

"von" can also be translated as "from" but unlike "aus" it is not used for things that were once inside something, but rather just that it is in a different place than before. It is "from there". "Von" points at the position where something was. "Zu" is the opposite pointing at the position where something will be.

**Ich komme vom Bäcker. -
I am coming from the bakery.**

The preposition "von" points at the bakery from where "ich" is coming. Also it is important to note that "vom" is a contraction of "von dem", which means if you are trying to use adjectives after that, you use the ones that normally are behind definite articles. Even though you can't see the article, it is still there in the contraction.

**Ich gehe zum Bäcker. -
I am going to the bakery.**

"zu" points at the bakery to where "ich" is going. Again there is a contraction of "zu" and "dem" in this sentence.

**Morgen soll ich einen Brief
von meiner Brieffreundin bekommen. -
I am supposed to get a letter from my penpal tomorrow.**

If I used "aus" in this sentence instead of "von", It would mean that the letter was once inside of your penpal. Since that is not what is meant here, I used "von".

**Wir fahren von unserem Haus zu deinem Haus. -
We are driving from our house to your house.**

This sentence is a bit more difficult for some to understand why we use "von" instead of "aus". The simplest way for me to explain it is that when we went from inside of the house to outside of the house, we weren't driving. The part explained in this sentence is the driving from the outside of one house to the outside of another. This means you can use them both in the same sentence to give more depth to the sentence.

**Wir gehen aus dem Haus und
fahren von unserem Haus zu deinem Haus. -
We are walking out of the house and
driving from our house to your house.**

Geben Sie mir bitte ein Stück von dem Kuchen! -
Give me a piece from/of the cake.

This sentence is actually a good transition example from the translation "from" to the other translation for "von", "of". It could be translated as a piece from the cake or a piece of the cake.

That's because the word "von" sometimes carries with it the idea of being a part of the whole or it can be used to show possession. This again goes back to the fact that it points where something was.

There are also a plethora of phrases in German, which use the preposition "von". In those sentences, the translation varies from the two options I have given you so far. This is when it is most helpful to use the definition I first saw on the "German is Easy" blog at yourdailygerman.com. "von" shows a point of origin without expressing any form of "exiting". I like this definition, as it shows a more precise definition that doesn't leave any ambiguity.

Die folgenden Sätze sind Beispiele
von dem deutschen Wort "von". -
The following sentences are examples
of the German word "von".

Herr Antrim erzählt
von einem Drachen mit roten Flügeln. -
Herr Antrim tells of a dragon with red wings.

Das ist das T-Shirt von meiner Tochter. -
This is the t-shirt of my daughter.

Von Büchern habe ich viel gelernt. -
I learned a lot from books.

You can also combine "von" and "dem" to get "vom". This works similarly to the other conjunctions we have seen before, but because of the close resemblance between -n and -m, instead of saying "vonm", we say "vom" as the contracted form.

Ich hole heute Brötchen frisch vom (von dem) Bäcker. - I am getting rolls fresh from the bakery today.

"außer" translates as either "except" or "besides". I sometimes use the translation "in addition to". It isn't nearly as common as "aus" and "von", but it is a dative preposition, so here it is in some examples.

Außer meinem Vater kommt auch noch meine Mutter zum Spiel. - Besides (In addition to) my father, my mother is also coming to the game.

Ich esse mein ganzes Mittagessen außer diesem Spargel. - I am eating my entire lunch except this asparagus.

Außer frischer Milch brauchen wir auch noch Kekse. - Besides fresh milk, we also need cookies.

"bei" is a bit difficult for some German learners, as it translates as a bunch of words that already have other prepositions assigned to them. Some translate it as "with", but "mit" exists. Some translate it as "near", but the word "nah" also exists. I generally translate it as "at", but that has a bunch of issues, too. The bottom line is that "bei" shows a static location. You can use it with stores, work, people's houses (not your own) and parties just to name a few.

Here are a few examples to help you get the idea.

Ich kaufe Lebensmittel bei Aldi. - I am buying groceries at Aldi.

For the record, it is NOT Aldi's. Aldi is not a dude's name unlike Kohl's, McDonald's and other stores, restaurants and companies that were derived from people's names. Aldi is short for Albrecht (a family name) Diskont (word for discount). The family's last name is not "Diskont", so please for the love of god stop saying "Aldi's". End rant.

**Es gibt heute Abend eine Party bei meinem Freund Paul. –
There is a party at my friend Paul's house this evening.**

**Mein Bruder ist gerade bei der Arbeit und kann nicht ans Handy gehen. –
My brother is currently at work and can't answer his phone (cell phone).**

**Heute kaufe ich Wurst beim (bei dem) Metzger. –
Today I am buying sausage at the butcher shop.**

Another contraction that we can make is the combination of "bei" and "dem", which become "beim".

**Bei kritischer Würdigung können wir das Ergebnis voraussagen. –
With critical assessment we can predict the outcome.**

This example is a bit more figurative, but it still carries the same translation and use.

You can also use "bei" with online places and sources of information. For example:

**Mein Vater liest all seine Nachrichten bei Fox News. –
My father reads all of his news on/at/from Fox News.**

**Herr Antrim hat eine Fan-Seite bei Facebook. –
Herr Antrim has a fan page on Facebook.**

"mit" is an easy one. It means "with" and is used exactly the same as the English preposition. For example:

**Mit frischem Gemüse macht man einen guten Salat. –
With fresh vegetables one makes a good salad.**

83

In this example I simply used the dative neuter ending on the adjective -em.

The most difficult part of this preposition is deciding whether to use "bei" or "mit" when you want to say "with" in English. The easy answer is that "mit" does not describe a location, but rather a connection, whereas "bei" always shows a location.

Ich **wohne** mit meinem Bruder. -
I **live** with my brother.
(**I live** in the same place as my brother.)

Ich **wohne** bei meinem Bruder. -
I **live** with my brother.
(**I live** at my brother's house.)

The sentence with "mit" indicates that both are equal, i.e. the home belongs to both. The other one indicates that the brother is either the tenant or owns the home, so he sets the rules.

Er **ist fertig** mit seiner Arbeit. -
He **is finished** with his work.

Er **ist** bei der Arbeit. -
He **is** at work.

Wir **spielen** Schach mit unseren Kindern. -
We **play** chess with our children.

This sentence uses "mit", as it is talking about the connection between the people represented by the pronoun "wir" and the children. They are all playing chess together. This next example uses "bei" and is talking about the location of the chess playing. They are playing "at our children's house".

Wir **spielen** Schach bei unseren Kindern. -
We **play** chess at our children's house.

"zu" can mean "at". The only instance when it translates as "at", however, is "zu Hause" (at home).

Ich bin die nächsten zwei Wochen zu Hause. - I am at home for the next two weeks.

In all other instances, the translation is "to". Generally speaking, this is used to express going in the direction of something. There are other prepositions that do this, however, so it is important to remember that you use "zu" with places that you can also use "von" when leaving. If you used the preposition "in" when you entered, you use "aus" when you exit. If you used "zu" when going there, you use "von" when leaving. For example:

Ich fahre zur Bank. - I am driving to the bank.

Ich komme von der Bank zurück nach Hause. - I am coming home from the bank.

Mein Bruder geht zu einem Freund. - My brother is going to a friend's house.

Mein Bruder kommt bald von seinem Freund nach Hause. - My brother will soon return from his friend's house.

In each of these I used "zu" to go towards that place and "von" to return. This pattern will almost always work. If you use "aus" to return from a place, you likely need to use "in" when going to it. This is a bit confusing sometimes, but it gets easier the more you see it.

You may have also noticed I used "nach Hause". This is an exception to the rules I have laid out. When going home, use "nach Hause". When you are already there, use "zu Hause".

**Was möchtest du zum (zu dem) Abendessen? -
What would you like for dinner?**

When talking about what you are having for a particular meal, use "zum" followed by that meal. As you probably have guessed, "zum" is a contraction of "zu" and "dem".

In addition to this contraction, you can also combine "zu" and "der" to get "zur". For example:

**Ich muss heute zur (zu der) Post. -
I have to go to the post office today.**

If you decide not to contract "zu dem" into "zum" or "zu der" into "zur" it draws extra attention to the article making it "that particular dinner" or "that particular post office". It is highly unlikely that this is the use you mean.

"nach" can also mean "to". It is used with cities, villages, states, countries and directions on a compass. Just don't forget the exception I mentioned before with "nach Hause".

**Im Sommer möchte ich nach Heidelberg fliegen.
-
In the summer I would like to fly to Heidelberg.**

**Meine Eltern fahren nach Deutschland. -
My parents are driving to Germany.**

**Gehen Sie nach Norden bis Sie das Restaurant finden. -
Go north until you find the restaurant.**

You can also use "nach" to express "after", as with time or an event.

Nach 3 Uhr arbeite **ich** nicht mehr. -
After 3 o'clock, **I** don't work anymore.

Nach dem Film gehen **wir** essen. -
After the film **we** are going out to eat.

"seit" is very similar, but translates as "since". The main difference is that "nach" indicates that some event or action occurred after another, but "seit" indicates that whatever the second action is continued for some time after that.

Ich arbeite **seit zwei Jahren bei dieser Firma.**
Nach Montag arbeite ich nicht mehr hier. -
I have worked **at this company for two years.**
After Monday **I** am not working here anymore.

Seit meiner Geburt heiße **ich Herr Antrim.** -
Since my birth **I** have been called **Herr Antrim.**

Seit dem Film schlafen **die Kinder.** -
The children have been sleeping **since the film.**

Seit den 90ern (Neunzigern) gibt **es**
keine gute Musik mehr. -
There hasn't been **any good music** **since the 90s.**

The last preposition in the dative case list is "gegenüber", which means "across from. You can use it like this.

Gegenüber dem Rathaus steht **ein Eiscafé.** -
Across from city hall **there is** **an ice cream café.**

Not only is "gegenüber" not very commonly used, but it is also a bit tricky, because it can be a postposition instead of a preposition, which is just a fancy way of saying that it gets put behind the noun it modifies rather than in front of it. For example:

Dem Rathaus gegenüber steht **ein Eiscafé**. – **Across from city hall** there is **an ice cream café**.

Again, the main thing to remember about dative prepositions is that they use the dative case. This means the articles, adjectives and pronouns all have to be in the dative case whenever you see one of these prepositions.

Don't get that twisted, however, and think that everything in the sentence becomes dative when you have a dative preposition. I hope that the amount of color you see in each of the example sentences makes that point clear. The noun or pronoun after the dative preposition is dative. Nothing else is affected by the preposition.

Complete exercises 4.14 - 4.17 in the workbook before continuing.

Two-Way Prepositions

There are nine prepositions that can switch between the accusative and dative cases. They are called two-way prepositions or "Wechselpräpositionen".

If you want to sing these prepositions in alphabetical order they fit really well with the song "The Battle Hymn of the Republic". If you don't care if they are in alphabetical order or not, you can sing them with "She'll be coming 'round the mountain" in the order you see them below. Again, if you want to hear me sing those songs, search for "German prepositions songs" on YouTube and look for the bow ties.

an - on (vertical)
auf - on (horizontal)
hinter - behind
in - into
neben - next to
über - over (above)
unter - under (below)
vor - in front of (before)
zwischen - between

♪ vor und hinter über unter neben an
2x
zwischen zwischen auf und in 2x
Wo ist Dativ.
Wohin is Akkusativ.
She'll be coming 'round
the mountain when she comes

The two-way prepositions are called this because they can use either the accusative or dative cases. It isn't a Schrödinger's preposition kind of situation. It is German. There is a method to this madness.

If the prepositional phrase describes a change in location, you need the accusative case within that phrase. If there is no change in location, you need the dative case.

Another way to phrase this is the difference between "wo" and "wohin". The question word "wo" means "where" and "wohin" means "to where". "Wo" indicates a stationary situation, which requires the dative case. "Wohin" indicates a change in location, which requires the accusative case.

Let's take the following sentence, as an example.

Das Kind krabbelt unter _____ Tisch. -
The child is crawling under the table.

Here we can use either the accusative or the dative case, but the connotation changes based on the case used. Basically it boils down to "was the child always under the table or is this expressing a change in location?"

If we say

Wo krabbelt das Kind? -
Where is the child crawling?

we answer with

Das Kind krabbelt unter dem Tisch. -
The child is crawling under the table.

This means that the child is crawling under the table, but never gets out from under the table. They are staying under the table, which means that they are not changing locations. This means that we have to use the dative case.

If we say

Wohin krabbelt das Kind? -
To where is the child crawling?

We answer with

Das Kind krabbelt unter den Tisch. -
The child is crawling under the table.

This means that the child started somewhere else and the destination is "under the table".

Depending upon the answer to the question of "wo" vs "wohin", there are certain situations where the direct object or lack thereof will not help you determine the correct case. While it is preferred to know the difference between "wo" and "wohin" in order to understand which case to use, there is a handy trick that works most of the time to figure it out without understanding that.

Certain verbs will lend themselves more to use the two-way prepositions with the accusative case and certain ones will mostly use the dative case. Generally speaking, if there is a direct object, you will more than likely use the accusative case. If there is not a direct object, you will use the dative case. WARNING: THIS IS A GENERALIZATION. IT DOESN'T ALWAYS WORK!

Use Accusative with Wechselpräpositionen	English	Use Dative with Wechselpräpositionen	English
legen	to lay	liegen	to lie
stellen	to put	stehen	to stand
setzen	to set	sitzen	to sit
hängen*	to hang	hängen*	to hang

This pattern is fascinating to me. For every verb on this list, the pattern holds true. The ones in the first column all require a direct object all of the time without exception. This means you have to "legen" something. You have to "stellen" something. You can't just "setzen". You have to "setzen" something.

All of the ones in the other category cannot have a direct object. They must all be used without a direct object. It isn't possible to use one with these four verbs.

All of the verbs in the first column are regular verbs in the past tenses. "Legen" becomes "legte" in the Präteritum tense and "gelegt" in the Perfekt. "Stellen" changes to "stellte" and "gestellt". "Setzen" - "setzte" - "gesetzt".

All of the verbs in the second category are irregular verbs in the past tenses. "Liegen" becomes "lag" and "gelegen". "Stehen" becomes "stand" and "gestanden". "Sitzen" - "saß" - "gesessen".

If you use a two-way preposition in a sentence with the first column of verbs, you almost always use the accusative case in that prepositional phrase. If you use a two-way preposition in a sentence with the second group of verbs, you almost always use the dative case within that prepositional phrase.

Short version: These verbs try as hard as they can to give you as many hints as possible to make sure you use the correct case if you encounter a two-way preposition near one of these verbs.

Let's start with the difference between "legen" and "liegen".

**Der Junge legt die Bonbons hinter das Regal. -
The boy puts the candy behind the shelf.**

This sentence has a direct object (die Bonbons) that is being put somewhere in a lying position. This is shown through the verb "legen". The "Bonbons" were not behind the shelf before, but as a result of the prepositional phrase "hinter das Regal", they are now behind the shelf.

The verb "liegen" shows the result after "legen" has been completed. In other words: "legen" shows the change in location, while "liegen" shows the new location.

**Die Bonbons liegen hinter dem Regal. -
The candy is behind the shelf.**

Here I used the dative case, because the "Bonbons" are not moving anymore. They are behind the shelf.

**Der Mann stellt die Action-Figur in das Regal. -
The man places the action figure on the shelf.**

The verb "stellen" places something in an upright position. In this example, the action figure was somewhere else and through the action of the verb "stellen" and the description of the prepositional phrase using "in" it was moved to a new location.

**Die Action-Figur steht im (in dem) Regal. -
The action figure is standing on the shelf.**

This sentence describes the new location of the action figure. It is in an upright position on the shelf. It is no longer moving, so we used the dative case.

Caution: Germans tend to say that you put things "in" shelves instead of "on" them. If you say "auf" in this situation, it means that they are "on top of" the shelf, where they more than likely shouldn't be.

**Das Mädchen setzt sich an den Tisch. -
The girl set herself down at the table.**

The verb "setzen" places something in a seated position. This means that the object of the sentence is likely something with legs, i.e. a person or an animal. In this sentence the one being "set" and the one doing the "setzen" is the same person, so we used the reflexive pronoun "sich". The change in location for this girl is then shown through the prepositional phrase and illustrated in the accusative case.

**Das Mädchen sitzt am (an dem) Tisch. -
The girl is sitting at the table.**

This sentence describes her location after the sitting process has been completed. It is a static location.

These sentences also showcase a very important distinction for the prepositions "auf" and "an". When you are sitting at a table, you use "an". When you are sitting on top of a table, use "auf".

**Der Mann hängt das Foto an die Wand. -
The man is hanging the photo onto the wall.**

Now let's get to the verb "hängen". You probably noticed that it was in both categories of verbs at the beginning of this section and there was a * next to the verb. That's because it all comes down to the direct object (or lack thereof).

This example has a direct object (das Foto) that is being moved from somewhere else to the wall. This change in location is shown in the accusative case with the preposition "an".

**Das Foto hängt an der Wand. -
The photo is hanging on the wall.**

This version does not have a direct object and describes the static location of the photo. You'll notice that our subject in the previous example was "the man" and the subject of this sentence is "the photo". That is because we are no longer focused on the movement, but rather the location.

The reason for the * next to the verb is because, technically, these are different verbs. In the present tense, they look the same. In the past tenses, however, they are different. They follow the same patterns as all of the other verbs in their respective clauses at the beginning of the chapter.

If "hängen" has a direct object, the past tense forms are regular. It becomes "hängte" and "gehängt". If "hängen" does not have a direct object, the past tense forms are irregular. It becomes "hing" and "gehangen".

93

If there is a direct object, the accusative case is used within the prepositional phrase with the two-way preposition. If there is no direct object, the dative case is used within the prepositional phrase with the two-way preposition.

On the surface this looks confusing, but it really is helpful in deciphering other sentences and the cases needed with the two-way prepositions. If there is a direct object, it is very likely that you need the accusative case. If there is no direct object, it is very likely that you need the dative case.

Die Frau stellt das Essen auf den Tisch. -
The woman is putting the food on the table.

There is a direct object in this sentence and we used the accusative case with the two-way preposition.

Das Essen steht auf dem Tisch. -
The food is on the table.

There is no direct object in this sentence and we used the dative case with the two-way preposition.

Caution: The verbs "(ver)senken" and "sinken" are the opposite of the general rule. Use the question words "wo" and "wohin" to help you here. They function in the same ways as the other pairs on our list in most ways. "Senken" requires a direct object and generally this means the two-way preposition will use the accusative case. "Sinken", by contrast, does not use a direct object and generally this means the two-way preposition uses the dative case.

In the following sentences, however, this rule does not hold true.

Das U-Boot versenkt den Zerstörer im (in dem) Meer. -
The submarine is sinking the destroyer in the sea.

Der Zerstörer sinkt in das Meer. -
The destroyer is sinking into the sea.

In cases like this, you need to follow the logic of "wo" and "wohin". Use dative with "wo" and accusative with "wohin".

Wo senkt das U-Boot den Zerstörer? Im Meer. -
Where is the submarine sinking the destroyer?
In the sea.

Wohin sinkt der Zerstörer? In das Meer. -
Into where is the destroyer sinking? Into the sea.

There are lots of situations in which the two-way prepositions can be a bit confusing. The main issue I have seen with my students is due to the Perfekt tense. When some students are taught the Perfekt tense they learn to use "sein' as a helping verb with motion verbs.

If it is a motion verb, it obviously changes the location of something, so we should use the accusative case with a two-way preposition with a verb like that, right? No. Actually, almost always it is the opposite of that.

Der Mann klettert an der Wand. -
The man is climbing on the wall.

The verb "klettern" uses the helping verb "sein" in the Perfekt tense. It changes the location. The important distinction, however, is that it changes the location of the subject. What is described in the prepositional phrase in this sentence is not about the change in location for the man. It is about the static location where his movement is taking place. You wouldn't say "To where is he climbing?" It is just "Where is he climbing?"

Die Kinder essen Abendessen an dem Tisch. -
The children are eating dinner at the table.

Here we have a direct object, but the two-way preposition requires the dative case. This is a similar explanation. The prepositional phrase is not describing a change in location. It is about the static location at which the children are eating.

**Das Kind wirft den Ball in das Haus. -
The child is throwing the ball into the house.**

Throwing something obviously changes its location. It makes sense that you would use the accusative case with a two-way preposition in this sentence. That only works, however, if the prepositional phrase describes the change in location.

**Das Kind wirft den Ball in dem Haus. -
The child is throwing the ball in the house.**

This time the prepositional phrase uses the dative case, because it isn't about the change in location for the ball. It is about the static location where the throwing is taking place.

**Ich habe das Blatt Papier auf den Tisch
in dem Wohnzimmer gelegt. -
I laid the piece of paper onto the table
in the living room.**

This sentence uses two different two-way prepositions with different cases for each. Break it down and think about what they are describing. "Auf den Tisch" describes the change in location for the piece of paper. Therefore we have to use the accusative case for that phrase.

The phrase "in dem Wohnzimmer", however, describes the location in which the placing of the paper takes place. A simpler version would be to say that it describe where the table is located. This requires the dative case.

**Ich bin mit meinem Hund
in meinem Auto nach Chicago gefahren. -
I drove to Chicago with my dog in my car.**

Everything about this sentence screams change in location. The verb "fahren" means "to drive", which is usually a change in location. The destination is given in the phrase "nach Chicago". What is described with the phrase "in meinem Auto", however, is not a change in location. It is the static location of the dog throughout the trip. He is in the car. He never leaves the car.

You can do these kinds of analysis with all sorts of sentences with two-way prepositions.

**Das Flugzeug ist über die Wolke geflogen. -
The airplane flew over the cloud.**

There was a small cloud and the plane went from one side of it to the other side. It changed the location. Therefore we need the accusative case.

**Das Flugzeug ist über der Wolke geflogen. -
The airplane flew over the cloud.**

All of the flying is taking place above the cloud. It requires the dative case. It really comes down to "what do you mean to say". You can be super precise with your language in German.

**Mein Bruder ist in den Bergen gewandert. -
My brother hiked in the mountains.**

This sentence indicates that your brother is doing some hiking and that action is taking place in the mountains.

**Mein Bruder ist in die Berge gewandert. -
My brother hiked into the mountains.**

This sentence indicates that your brother is hiking from somewhere that is not consider "in the mountains" and ends up "in the mountains".

**Ich setze mich auf dem Tisch hin,
da mein Stuhl schon auf dem Tisch ist. -
I set myself down on the table,
because my chair is already on the table.**

In this sentence I purposefully confused you. The verb "hinsetzen" is usually used with the two-way preposition using the accusative case, but that is because the act of setting oneself down indicates a change of position from "not sitting" to "sitting".

In this sentence, however, the entire action of setting oneself down happens on top of the table, as the chair onto which the person is setting themselves is on the table. Of course this is an extreme example of the distinction between when to use the accusative and when to use the dative, but this it might help you to see things like this.

In previous chapters I have mentioned contractions that can be made with certain prepositions and articles. There are several that can be made with the two-way prepositions, too. They are listed below.

an + das = ans
an + dem = am
in + das = ins
in + dem = im

While I have shown you a wide variety of examples so far with these prepositions, I want to make sure that I have at least one example of each preposition. Here is one more example with each of the two-way prepositions.

**Ich habe am fünfzehnten November Geburtstag. -
I have my birthday on November 15th.**

You don't have to use "an" literally. When you are talking about dates, you say "am" followed by the ordinal number for the date.

**Er ist auf dem Weg nach Hause. -
He is on his way home.**

This one is sometimes confusing. He is changing his location, but the action of the sentence continues to take place in the same place, "on the path".

Er geht auf dem Gehweg. - He is walking on the sidewalk.

Er geht auf den Gehweg. - He walks onto the sidewalk.

In these two examples you can see this illustrated with the difference between "on" and "onto" in English. When he is continually walking on the sidewalk, we use the dative and when he changes his location onto the sidewalk, we use the accusative case.

Ich stehe auf diese Band. - I like this band.

Ich stehe auf dieser Band. - I am standing on this band.

This is one weird distinction. If you use the accusative case, like I did in the first example here, you mean "I like this band." If you use the dative case, it is no longer used figuratively and means you are literally standing on the band.

Der Junge versteckt sich hinter dem Schrank. - The boy is hiding (himself) behind the wardrobe.

This is another great example of when you need to ask "wo" or "wohin". Honestly, it kind of depends. If you mean to describe the action of moving into position behind the wardrobe, you would use the accusative case. The example I gave, however, shows the location of his hiding place.

Der Zug kommt im Bahnhof an. - The train arrives in the train station.

Again, ask yourself "wo" or "wohin". You would say "Where is the train arriving?" While you would use "in den Bahnhof" if it were driving into the train station, this sentence uses the verb "arrives", which is a different meaning. The "arrival" takes place at a static location, so we have to use the dative case. The same is true when you land a plane or park a car. Both use the dative case with these kinds of phrases.

In den letzten Jahren hat er sich gar nicht verändert. - He hasn't changed (himself) at all in the last few years.

You can use "in" with time, too. When you do, you use the dative case. The bottom line is that it is a static location within time. It isn't a literal location, but more of a temporal one. The lack of a change in location is what matters here. Use the dative case with time and two-way prepositions.

Das Buch liegt neben der Tasse. -
The book is lying next to the cup.

Wow. Would you look at that? It is a pretty straight forward static location sentence. Bet you didn't expect to see any more easy sentences in this book. This one uses the dative case with "neben", because the verb "liegen" describes the static location of the book.

Ich lege das Buch neben die Tasse. -
I lay the book next to the cup.

This sentence uses the accusative case with the preposition "neben" because we are changing the location of the book with the verb "legen".

Die Kuh springt über den Mond. -
The cow jumps over the moon.

That's right! Nursery rhymes can teach you about German grammar too. The cow went from somewhere else to the position over the moon, which shows a change in location, so we have to use the accusative case here.

Die Kuh steht über dem Frosch. -
The cow is standing over the frog.

Everyone knows the nursery rhyme about the cow standing over the frog, right? No? Well, this sentence is still a good example of using the dative case. We are describing a static location of the cow over the frog, even if it isn't a nursery rhyme.

Meine Katze spricht mit mir über den Tod hinaus. -
My cat talks to me from beyond the grave.

Even I'll admit this is an odd use of the two-way prepositions, but this is an interesting one. Because your cat in this example is projecting their speech from the other side of the grave to our side you have to use the accusative case to show that they are crossing that threshold. We do this through the preposition "über".

Ich möchte nicht mehr unter anderen Menschen **sein.** -
I don't want to be among other people **any more.**

This one uses a kind of fixed phrase. The idea of being among other people is a more figurative use of the preposition "unter", but it still fits the same requirements. It is a static location. You just aren't literally under other people.

Mein Mann besitzt eine Insel vor der Küste von Argentinien. -
My husband owns an island off the coast of Argentina.

The preposition "vor" doesn't always have to be translated as "before" or "in front of". In this sentence I used the word "off" in English. Here, "vor" is translated as "off" because it indicates proximity to the coast.

Er stellt die Vase zwischen die Säulen. -
He puts the vase between the columns.

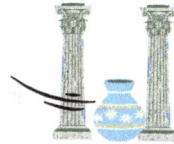

Die Vase steht zwischen den Säulen. -
The vase is standing between the columns.

You can use the preposition "zwischen" literally to mean "between" like I did in these two examples. Again, one shows a change in location with the accusative case and the other shows a static location with the dative case.

Manchmal muss man zwischen den Zeilen **lesen.** -
Sometimes you have to read between the lines.

This is a very common phrase in both languages and requires you to ask "wo" or "wohin" again. The location of the reading is between the lines, so the dative case has to be used.

Just remember the next time you are trying to figure out if a Wechselpräposition uses the accusative or dative case, ask yourself if you are trying to express a change in location with that preposition or not. If you are, use accusative. If not, use dative.

Complete exercises 4.18 - 4.20 in the workbook before continuing.

Possession with "dem sein"

While we will examine possession in great detail in the next chapter, there is one way to express possession in German that uses a combination of nouns with the dative case. It is not officially recognized by grammar nerds and most grammar books, but I promised to help you master the case system in German, so I will not be leaving it out of this book.

Basically what happens is you use the dative case to say who is in possession of something. Then you use a possessive article (more on those later) that matches the case and gender of the noun being possessed with that noun. None of that probably made sense when you read it, so let's try an example to get our bearings.

Hast du dem Vater seine Autoschlüssel gesehen? - Have you seen your father's car keys?

If you are confused and scratching your head right now, that is a perfectly natural reaction to seeing this weirdness. Let's see if I can break it down so it makes sense.

The subject of the sentence is "du", which gives us our nominative case thing and the conjugation of the verb, "hast". The keys are the things being seen, which makes them the direct object and accusative. We used the possessive article with a plural ending to end up with "seine". To define to whom "his" refers, we added an extra noun, "dem Vater".

It is essentially a possessive in two parts. The possessive article "sein" matches the gender of the father. In other words, we didn't say "her" in this sentence, because the father is masculine. Because the noun that follows the possessive article is plural, we added an -e in the accusative case.

The dative case is used with the father to show he is neither the subject nor the direct object, but is instead indirectly associated with the information in the sentence. He is the "him" to which "his" points.

Das ist dem Mädchen seine Schaufel, gib sie zurück! - That is the girl's shovel, give it back!

This sentence used a very similar setup. Both "das" and "seine Schaufel" are written in the nominative case, as "das" is the subject and "seine Schaufel" is a predicate noun or a restating of the subject after the verb. The stuff after the comma is just there as extra information, but only includes an accusative pronoun "sie" to refer back to the shovel and functions as the direct object of that clause.

The word "seine" is used again, but this time it is because we used a neuter noun "das Mädchen", which requires a neuter possessive article, "sein". In conversation, you might hear people use the more natural gender and say "ihre", as this would mean "her" instead of "its".

The dative case was used with the girl to show that she is the "her" to which the "sein" is pointing. Again, the dative one goes first and then there is a possessive article and the noun being possessed.

Steuern sind den Leuten ihr Geld und müssen für die Leute ausgegeben werden. - Taxes are the people's money and must be spent on the people.

This example is a bit more complex, but you can really just look at the first part (before the comma) and focus on that. Both "Steuern" and "ihr Geld" are in red, as they are the subject and predicate noun just as in the previous example.

"Leute" is usually the plural form, but since this is used in the dative case, we used the article "den" and added an -n to the end of the noun. These people are the "they" to whom the "ihr" (their) points. It is "their money". Whose money? The people's.

In a small bit of good news, this sort of phrasing is generally frowned upon in academic settings and is rarely if ever seen in written works. It is however the title of a book that annoys grammar nerds, "Der Dativ ist dem Genitiv sein Tod" (The dative is the death of the genitive). It is more of a "nice to know" kind of thing than a "must know". For all of these reasons there are no exercises for this topic in the workbook.

Dative Case Review

To bring this chapter all together, the dative case is used for indirect objects, which are the person (or on rare occasions an animal) that receives the direct object. If something is "verbed" in the direction of someone else, that someone else is the indirect object.

The dative case also shows up when we use certain phrases, certain verbs and certain prepositions. There are even prepositions that can either be accusative or dative based on the change in location or the lack thereof. It makes itself known through the -m at the end of masculine and neuter articles, -r for feminine and -n for plural.

To practice what you have learned in this chapter, use chapter 4 in the companion workbook or use the link below to access the digital materials for this chapter.

Due to the amount of information covered in this chapter, there are several pages of exercises for these topics in the workbook, but if you were following the recommendations from the beginning of this book, you would have been doing the exercises throughout the chapter instead of waiting until the end of the chapter to start the exercises.

Extra materials for this chapter:
https://www.germanwithantrim.com/mastering-cases/

Genitive Case Basics

The final case in the system is the genitive case. The genitive case is primarily used for possession. Just like in the dative case, the feminine forms are "der" and "einer" for genitive. The genitive case is also used for a variety of other uses including indefinite time, certain verbs, special genitive construction and certain prepositions. You'll learn about all of these things in this chapter.

Possessive Basics

While English possessive forms have adopted an apostrophe between the noun and the -s, the German versions have not.

It has become popular in recent years, however, to include possessive apostrophes in German business names, but this is unaffectionately referred to as the "Deppenapostroph" (fool's apostrophe), as it is not standard German.

For entertainment, visit: deppenapostroph.info to see real life examples of German speakers not understanding when or if they need to add an apostrophe in German. It makes me smile.

To show that someone is in possession of something or that they own that thing when using their name, simply add -s to the end of their name. If the name already ends in -s or -z, simply add an apostrophe after the letter, without adding another -s.

Bobs Boot - Bob's Boat

Klaus' Haus -
Klaus's house or Klaus' house*

*In English it is acceptable to include the additional "S" or leave it out when the name already ends with an "S". I personally prefer the version without the extra "S", but it is left up to the individual.

When there is not a proper name, you need to put the person (or thing) possessing something *after* the object they possess. While you can show possession using the dative preposition "von", you should remove this "von" and use the genitive case to show this possession instead, as this is the preferred formation.

Genitive - it takes the
'**von**' (fun) out of things.
- Herr Antrim

die Farbe von dem Hemd - die Farbe des Hemdes
the color of the shirt - the color of the shirt

Definite Articles

Below is a chart for the definite articles. This time it includes all four cases: nominative, accusative, dative and genitive.

	Masculine	Feminine	Neuter	Plural
Nominative	der	die	das	die
Accusative	den	die	das	die
Dative	dem	der	dem	den (n)
Genitive	des (s)	der	des (s)	der

If you continue the mnemonic device pattern that we have used so far and look at the last letter of each word, you end up with the full mnemonic device as: RESE (ressa), NESE (nessa), MRMN (Mr. Mann or Merman), SRSR (sir sir).

The (s) under masculine and neuter forms in the genitive case are meant to show that the noun will usually require an "S" or "ES" in the genitive case.

One more reminder that these endings are the same for all of the der-words including: dieser, jeder, manche, solche, alle, welcher and beide. The chart below shows what it would look like, if you added all of the endings to the word "dieser".

	Masculine	Feminine	Neuter	Plural
Nominative	dieser	diese	dieses	diese
Accusative	diesen	diese	dieses	diese
Dative	diesem	dieser	diesem	diesen (n)
Genitive	dieses (s)	dieser	dieses (s)	dieser

With masculine or neuter in the genitive case you need to add -s or -es to the end of the noun. If the noun has one syllable, add -es. If the noun has more than one syllable, just add -s. To count syllables, put your hand on the bottom of your chin. The number of times your chin moves is the number of syllables the word has.

der Hut des Mannes -
the hat of the man

die Farbe des Autos -
the color of the car

It is important to note that you don't add -s or -es for feminine or plural nouns. The article is "der" for these two forms, which is usually enough of a hint that you don't need an -s anywhere.

die Farbe der Krawatte -
the color of the tie

die Telefonnummer der Nachbarn -
the phone number of the neighbors

Contact Us
867-5309

One cool aspect of the genitive case is that the placement of the case is not fixed within the sentence. As long as it shows up behind the thing being possessed, the genitive case can be used behind the subject, object or even the object of a preposition. This gives us the ability to show ridiculous examples like the ones below.

Die Ehefrau des Mannes gibt
dem Sohn des Ehepaars den Schlüssel des Autos. -
The wife of the man gives
the son of the couple the key of the car.
(The man's wife gives the couple's son the car key.)

This sentence has a lot going on. The first use of the genitive case is after the subject. The wife is the one doing something. She is giving something. This makes her the subject and nominative. The man is the one to whom she belongs. She is "the wife of the man". To show this in German, we use the genitive case for the man.

The second use of the genitive case shows up after the dative object "dem Sohn". The son belongs to the couple, which puts the couple in the genitive case.

The third use of the genitive case in this sentence is after "den Schlüssel", which is the thing being given to the son, i.e. the direct object, which is accusative. The key belongs to the car, which makes the car the genitive object.

The noun "Mann" is masculine, so the article in the genitive case is "des" and there is also an -es added to the noun. "Ehepaar" and "Auto" are both neuter nouns, which means they also use the article "des" in these sentences and add -s to the end of the noun.

While the word "Mann" has one syllable and therefore requires -es at the end of the noun, both "Ehepaar" and "Auto" have multiple syllables. These means these two nouns only get an -s at the end of the noun rather than an -es.

Die Farbe des Kellers gefällt
dem Mann des Hauses nicht. -
The man of the house doesn't like
the color of the basement.
(The man of the house doesn't like
the basement's color.)

This sentence follows a similar pattern. We have a subject highlighted in red "die Farbe". This is the thing that is not pleasing to the man. "Mann" is the object of the dative verb "gefallen", which makes the article "dem". Both the color and the man belong to something. The color belongs to the basement and the man belongs to the house. This puts both of those in the genitive case.

Since the basement is a masculine noun with more than one syllable, we use the article "des" and add -s to the end of the noun to get "des Kellers".

Since the house is a neuter noun with only one syllable, we use the article "des" and add -es to the end of the noun to get "des Hauses".

**Wir mieten den größten Konzertsaal der Stadt
für die Geburtstagsparty der Frau. -
We are renting the largest concert hall of the city
for the birthday party of the woman.
(We are renting the city's largest concert hall
for the woman's birthday party.)**

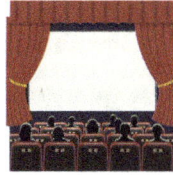

In this sentence we have a subject, "wir", a direct object, "den größten Konzertsaal", and a prepositional phrase that starts with "für". I left the subject alone in this sentence, but the two accusative objects within the sentence gained a genitive partner.

The "Konzertsaal" belongs to the city, so the city is in the genitive case. Since "Stadt" is a feminine noun, I used the article "der". Don't forget that the noun does not get an ending added to it for feminine and plural nouns. The "Geburtstagsparty" belongs to the woman, which gives us the same genitive article "der" for "der Frau".

**Die Fragen der Prüfungen
waren nicht sehr schwierig. -
The questions of the tests were not very difficult.
(The test's questions were not very difficult.)**

For our last example with definite articles, I kept things pretty simple. There is only one genitive part, which is showing that the questions belong to the tests. This puts the tests in the genitive case. Since they are plural, we use the article "der" and there is nothing added to the end of the noun.

Complete exercise 5.1 in the workbook before continuing.

Indefinite Articles

Since by now you surely know what indefinite articles are, as I have already covered them two other times in this book, I'm just going to include the chart below for the indefinite articles with all four cases: nominative, accusative, dative and genitive.

	Masculine	Feminine	Neuter	Plural
Nominative	ein	eine	ein	(k)eine
Accusative	einen	eine	ein	(k)eine
Dative	einem	einer	einem	(k)einen (n)
Genitive	eines (s)	einer	eines (s)	(k)einer

Again, don't forget that (s) indicates that the noun will also add -s or -es if possible.

And to make sure that you remember that possessive adjectives or the negative ein-word, "kein", can also be used with these same endings, here is an example chart using the possessive adjective "mein".

	Masculine	Feminine	Neuter	Plural
Nominative	mein	meine	mein	meine
Accusative	meinen	meine	mein	meine
Dative	meinem	meiner	meinem	meinen (n)
Genitive	meines (s)	meiner	meines (s)	meiner

Die Frau meines Bruders verkauft
dem Sohn eines Lehrers die Tür eines Käfers. -
The wife of my brother is selling
the son of a teacher the door of a Beetle (VW).
(My brother's wife is selling
a teacher's son a Beetle door.)

In our first example, there are three uses of the genitive case with ein-words. The first is after our subject, "die Frau". The wife is the one doing something, which makes her the subject and nominative. She is the wife of my brother, which means "mein Bruder" becomes "meines Bruders" to show possession in the genitive case.

The thing being sold in this sentence is "die Tür". This is accusative, as it is the direct object of the sentence. The door belongs to a Beetle (as in the Volkswagen car). To show this possession we change "ein Käfer" into "eines Käfers" in the genitive case.

The person to whom the door is being sold is our indirect object in the dative case, "dem Sohn". The son is the son of a teacher, which requires us to change "ein Lehrer" to "eines Lehrers" to show possession in the genitive case.

**Die Fenster eines Hauses können
die Effizienz eines Heizungssystems beeinflussen. -
The windows of a house can influence
the efficiency of a heating system.
(The house windows can influence
a heating system's efficiency.)**

In this example we have two uses of the genitive case. The first is after the subject to show that the windows belong to a house, so we say "eines Hauses" instead of "ein Haus". The second use tells us that the efficiency belongs to the heating system, which gives us the genitive version "eines Heizungssystems" instead of "ein Heizungssystem".

**Die Geschichte seiner Flucht ist sehr beeindruckend. -
The story of his escape is very impressive.
(His escape story is very impressive.)**

This time we again did not use a person who owns something, but rather a relationship between two objects. If you haven't picked up on it yet, most of the time when we say "of the" or "of a" in English, we need something genitive in the German version.

**Das Auto meiner Eltern steht
vor dem Haus meiner Freunde. -
The car of my parents is standing
in front of the house of my friends.
(My parents' car is standing in front
of my friends' house.)**

In our last example we have two plural nouns being used in the genitive case. Both of their articles end with -er, as this is what happens to plural nouns in the genitive case.

Complete exercises 5.2 and 5.3 in the workbook before continuing.

Possessive Pronouns, Adjectives and Articles

Since the genitive case is used to express possession, the possessive adjectives such as "mein", "dein", "sein" and so on, are technically a kind of genitive pronoun. They replace the person or thing that is in possession of something. This allows us to say "seine Krawatte instead of "Bobs Krawatte".

They are officially called "possessive adjectives". This leads to some confusion, as they act more like articles than adjectives. Even the adjectives used after these words act like adjectives after ein-words.

For this reason, I usually refer to these things ("mein", "dein", "sein", etc) as possessive articles, even though this term is not widely accepted.

To complicate this matter even further, there are times when you would use the possessive pronouns as real pronouns, meaning that they replace a noun. In English we can say things like "mine", "his" or "yours". These are the same type of things in German.

True genitive pronouns do exist, but they are so incredibly rare that most Germans would balk at their use. There will always be another way to phrase the sentence you want to say without using a genitive pronoun, but this wouldn't be a book called "Mastering the German Case System" if I didn't at least mention them.

While I talked about all of the other pronouns on the chart below already in this book, I want to focus on the first and last columns (nominative and genitive). You already know the nominative pronouns, they are the ones that show up in conjugation charts and have been used in countless examples in this book already. The genitive ones are the ones I have been alluding to throughout this book, but this is finally the point at which I teach them all to you.

Nom	Akk	Dat	Gen
ich	mich	mir	mein
du	dich	dir	dein
er	ihn	ihm	sein
sie	sie	ihr	ihr
es	es	ihm	sein

Nom	Akk	Dat	Gen
wir	uns	uns	unser
ihr	euch	euch	euer
sie	sie	ihnen	ihr
Sie	Sie	Ihnen	Ihr

The words listed in the genitive case are the words to which you would add the ein-word endings that were listed in the previous section of this chapter. The 1st person possessive word "mein" can be "meine", "meiner", "meinem", or "meines" among others. This all depends on the case and gender of the noun that they are modifying.

While those are the normal ones, the official possessive pronouns are those same words, but with a slight change to the endings list. If you are using these words as true genitive possessive pronouns, you need the endings listed in the example chart below with "mein".

	Masculine	Feminine	Neuter	Plural
Nominative	mein**er**	mein**e**	mein**s**	mein**e**
Accusative	mein**en**	mein**e**	mein**s**	mein**e**
Dative	mein**em**	mein**er**	mein**em**	mein**en** (n)
Genitive	mein**es** (s)	mein**er**	mein**es** (s)	mein**er**

Let's try a few examples to see what these two categories of words look like in sentences.

Das **ist** mein Hut. **-** That **is** my hat.
Du **hast** meinen Hut. **-** You **have** my hat.

In the first sentence here, "mein" is simply a possessive article. It does not have an ending, as it is followed by a masculine noun in the nominative case. In the second sentence, we have another possessive article that has -en added to the end of it, because it is followed by a masculine noun in the accusative case.

Nein, das **ist** meiner. **-** No, this **is** mine.
Du **hast** deinen. **-** You **have** yours.

In these examples we see two examples of the possessive pronouns. Even though the case and gender of the possessive words are the same between these examples and the previous set of examples, the ending on the first one changed, because we no longer have the noun after the possessive. This is how we can tell that this is a possessive pronoun and not a possessive article.

Ich **habe** ein Hemd **gefunden.** -
I **found** a shirt.
Das **ist** meins. **-** That **is** mine.

In this example we start with a simple ein-word in the first sentence. This establishes the item to which the pronoun in the second sentence refers. Since "ein Hemd" is a neuter noun, we have to use the neuter endings for articles and pronouns.

In the first sentence, the noun is present and in the accusative case, so we use the article endings, which in this case is no ending. In the second sentence we used the pronoun version. Since this is representing a neuter noun, we had to add an -s to the end of the pronoun.

As a quick side note, technically the ending for the pronoun in the second sentence (and in the nominative and accusative cases in my chart) should be -es, but I don't know anyone who actually says that or cares in everyday conversation. If you use "meins" or "meines" most people will ignore it entirely. It doesn't really matter which one you choose.

Wo ist dein Schuh? Meiner ist da. -
Where is your shoe? Mine is there.

This set of sentences works similarly. In the first version we see the possessive article followed by the noun, "Schuh". Since the shoe is masculine and in the nominative case in this sentence, we do not need an ending on the article. In the second sentence, we used -er at the end, because there is no noun present, which means we are working with a possessive pronoun.

Hast du deinen Schuh? Ja, ich habe meinen. -
Do you have your shoe? Yes, I have mine.

This is pretty much the same scenario, but because the accusative masculine form requires -en no matter what, we don't care which one is a pronoun and which one is an article. For the record, however, the first sentence uses a possessive article and the second uses a possessive pronoun.

Hast du einen Schuh? Ja.
Was machst du dann mit meinem? -
Do you have a shoe? Yes.
What are you doing with mine then?

Keeping with our shoe theme, this sentence uses a possessive pronoun in the dative case. Even if the possessive article was used instead, the ending would still be -em, as there is no difference between the endings charts for this case.

Genitive Question Words

As you probably have guessed, there is a genitive question word for people. It is "wessen". This word is basically the same as "whose" in English. It is used to ask about the person who owns a thing or to whom something belongs. While you probably should answer this question word with something involving the genitive case, because of the nature of the preposition "von", you can get around using the genitive case in these answers.

Wessen Hemd ist das? - Whose shirt is that?
Das ist das Hemd meines Bruders. -
That is the shirt of my brother.

In this sentence we are inquiring about the owner of the shirt. Therefore we need the question word "wessen". We simply add this question word in front of the noun and then continue the rest of our sentence as normal.

In my answer to this question I chose to use the genitive case with "meines Bruders" after the shirt. This shows us the continuation of the pattern I keep mentioning, but slightly modified. The last letter of "wer", "wen" and "wem" match the der-word endings for masculine nouns in their respective cases or the last letter of the masculine personal pronoun in each case.

The question word "wessen" does not end with -s, but the articles for masculine nouns in the genitive case do. So how can I claim it still has the same pattern? Well, the two S's in the middle of "wessen" can both be seen in the answer. The first one is at the end of the article and the second is at the end of the noun.

Wessen Buch liest du? - Whose book are you reading?
Ich lese F. Scott Fitzgeralds Buch. -
I am reading F. Scott Fitzgerald's book.

Here is one more example using "wessen", so you get another look at it before we move on. This time I chose to use a person's name with the genitive case, so the word order looks a bit different, but the general idea is still the same. I asked to whom the book belongs. Then I answered with a person in the genitive case.

I mentioned the idea of letters at the end of the question words matching articles and pronouns several times in this chapter, but there is one word or warning I need to say before we get to the next chapter. Just because the question word endings match these articles and pronouns does not mean that the answer has to be masculine.

I can't tell you how many times my students have made the false assumption that "wem" is always answered with a sentence that says "dem" somewhere in it. It does not. I simply meant to show the pattern that can be there, not to say that the pattern has to be there. If a feminine noun is the answer to the question, by all means use the feminine articles or pronouns. The examples in this chapter are just that. Examples.

Complete exercise 5.4 in the workbook before continuing.

Indefinite Time

In the accusative case chapter I mentioned that specific time is used in the accusative case. I alluded to the idea that you would use a different case when talking about a less specific time. That is reserved for the genitive case. It is a more abstract version of time. Let's compare the time in the following examples.

Jeden Tag esse ich Eis. - Every day I eat ice cream.
Eines Tages werde ich aufhören. - Someday I will stop.

In the first sentence we used a specific day "every day", which requires the accusative case, as it is not abstract. In the second sentence, I had to use the genitive form "eines Tages" for "one day", because we don't know which day that will be. We just know it isn't today. Also, let's be honest, I'm never going to stop eating ice cream. It is delicious.

Als Gregor Samsa eines Morgens erwachte,
fand er sich zu einem ungeheuren Ungeziefer verwandelt. -
When Gregor Samsa awoke one morning,
he found he had been turned into a monstrous bug.

In one of the weirdest cross-cultural literature examples I know of we find this example at the very beginning. The story is "die Verwandlung" (English: The Metamorphosis) by Franz Kafka. Kafka is purposefully vague as to when this occurred, because he is purposefully vague on a bunch of other things throughout the story, so why would it make sense for him to be specific here? All of this is to say we use the genitive case for "one morning", because we don't know when this morning was, but it was "eines Morgens".

Complete exercise 5.5 in the workbook before continuing.

Special Genitive Construction

Just as there were certain phrases that required the dative case, there are others that require the genitive case. While in the dative examples, we mostly stuck to describing relationships through the dative case involving describing the people involved in the sentence, the genitive ones are almost all adjectives (words that describe people, places and things) and can almost always be translated with "of" somewhere in the sentence in English.

**Er ist seines Erfolgs gewiss. -
He is confident of his success.**

The adjective "gewiss" requires the use of the genitive case to show "of what" one is confident. So while the adjective itself does not have a case associated with it, as cases are reserved for nouns and their friends, the noun that is connected to this adjective through context requires the genitive case.

**Ich bin mir seines Verrats bewusst. -
I am aware of his betrayal.**

The adjective "bewusst" requires the genitive case to be applied to whatever noun is connected to it through context. In English, we represent this context and connection through the use of the word "of". Whatever shows up after "of" in the English translation must be written in the genitive case in the German version.

**Dieser Mann ist des Mordes schuldig. -
This man is guilty of the murder.**

Not only does "schuldig" require the genitive case, but also "unschuldig" also requires it. This means it does not matter if he is guilty or innocent, the murder still has to be written with the genitive case, because of these adjectives.

**Mein Schwiegervater fliegt immer erster Klasse. -
My father-in-law always flies first class.**

This example is the first of a few that don't use just adjectives. This one is actually just "1st class". It is always used in the genitive case. It is called "genitivus partitivus", which means "genitive of part", as they are traveling as part of the first class. For this reason, it is always "erster Klasse" and not "erste Klasse" unless you are simply talking about the designation and not expressing how one is traveling.

Seine Tochter ist heute guter Laune. - His daughter is in a good mood today.

This sentence uses similar logic. If you are talking about a good mood or bad mood, it is written with -er at the end of the adjective to indicate the genitive case.

Wir sind festen Glaubens, dass wir gewinnen werden. - We are of firm faith, that we will win.

Here is one last adjective-noun combination that uses the genitive case. It goes back to the pattern of translating the genitive case with "of" somewhere in the sentence.

Complete exercise 5.6 in the workbook before continuing.

Genitive Verbs

Just as there are dative verbs, there are genitive verbs. If I weren't writing this book, I would not know any of them. So if you skip this part of the book, you will not be missing anything terribly important and you won't offend me. In the interest of being thorough, however, I am going to teach them to you so you can confuse your friends in Germany.

A short list of these verbs would include: sich enthalten (to refrain from, abstain from), sich bedienen (to make use of, employ), gedenken (to think of, commemorate), and bedürfen (to be in need of).

This is by no means an exhaustive list, but as I mentioned before, there is practically a zero percent chance that you will ever need to use a genitive verb in conversation. Just to make sure you are well educated, however, let's see some example sentences with these verbs.

sich enthalten - to refrain from, abstain
Der Politiker enthält sich der Stimme. -
The politician abstains from voting.

This verb is even more irritating, because of the reflexive pronoun (covered later in this book), which makes people think that the other object should be accusative. Instead the reflexive pronoun remains in the accusative case and the extra noun is the genitive object.

To make matters worse, there is already a verb "enthalten", which is "to contain" and works like any other verb. The object would use the accusative case, just like any other normal verb with a direct object.

sich bedienen - to make use of
Bill Nye bedient sich des Wissens um uns zu begeistern. -
Bill Nye makes use of knowledge to inspire us.

Again, we see the reflexive pronoun "sich" in the accusative case and the other object of the sentence in the genitive case. This verb also already exists without the genitive component. When used without the genitive piece, it simply means "to help oneself".

gedenken - to think of, commemorate
Die ganze Nation gedenkt des Jahrestags des Anschlags.
-
The entire nation commemorates
the anniversary of the attack.

This is one of the few times that you might actually encounter a genitive verb in the wild. When something is dedicated to a particular event, it often bears the name of the event in the genitive case, because it is a "Gedenkstätte" (memorial). Even the word for a memorial has part of the verb in it, "Gedenk-".

bedürfen - to be in need of
Sie bedarf nur eines Trostes. -
She is only in need of comfort/consolation.

There are so many other ways you could phrase this same sentiment without resorting to a genitive verb. It is just so odd to even be writing this sentence out. Genitive verbs are rare unicorns that are best left to professionals.

Due to the specialized nature of these verbs, there are no exercises in the workbook for them.

Genitive Prepositions

Genitive prepositions are exactly what the name implies. They are prepositions that require the object that follows to be used in the genitive case. There are upwards of 16 of these prepositions, but there are usually 4 or 5 listed in most German textbooks, as these are the most commonly used ones. I'll start with those in this chapter and then move on to the others.

German	English
anstatt	instead of
anstelle	in place of
trotz	in spite of, despite
während	during
wegen	because of

Anstatt eines Autos kaufe ich ein Fahrrad.
-
Instead of a car, I buy a bike.

Anstatt eines Hundes bekomme ich eine Katze. -
Instead of a dog, I get a cat.

As you can see with these two examples, the object that follows the preposition is in the genitive case, "eines Autos" and "eines Kuchens".

Der Junge isst einen Apfel statt eines Kuchens. -
The boy is eating an apple instead of a cake.

In this example I said "statt" without the "an" at the beginning. This is also an acceptable version of this preposition. The meaning doesn't change. It is just a personal preference if you want to say "statt" or "anstatt".

The preposition "anstelle" is very similar to "anstatt" and in many instances they can be interchangeable with each other. "Anstelle" is more closely translated with "in the place of", but the general idea is the same.

Ich kaufe eine Zeitschrift anstelle eines Buches. -
I am buying a magazine instead of a book.

The preposition "trotz" is used in a very similar way to the English phrase "in spite of" or "despite". It shows a juxtaposition of one thing vs the action taken. Basically "there is this circumstance" but "they did this anyway".

Trotz der Kälte steht er im Regen. -
In spite of the cold he is standing in the rain.

Trotz des schlechten Wetters spielen wir Fußball. -
In spite of the bad weather, we are playing soccer.

Die Lehrerin wiederholt
die Anweisungen trotz des Lärms. -
The teacher repeats the instructions despite the noise.

"Während" is a bit tricky, because there is also the conjunction "während", which is used to express very similar concepts. The main thing to remember is that the preposition "während" is combined with a noun, while the conjunction "während" is combined with a subordinate clause.

Während des Spiel(e)s
habe ich mich verletzt. -
During the game, I injured myself.

Technically you are supposed to say "Spieles" for the genitive form of "Spiel", as it only has one syllable. Duden (the authority on all things German grammar) lists both "Spieles" and "Spiels", however, and "Spiels" sounds better to my internal "Sprachgefühl".

Während des Sturms gab es einen Stromausfall. -
During the storm there was a power outage.

**Ich bin während des Spiels eingeschlafen.
Wer hat gewonnen? -
I fell asleep during the game. Who won?**

In general, if you can translate the sentence into English with the word "while", you probably mean the conjunction and not the preposition. When "während" is used as a preposition, it is almost always translated as "during".

**Während ich ein Eis esse,
isst meine Schwester etwas Brokkoli. -
While I am eating ice cream,
my sister is eating some broccoli.**

This is an example of "während" used as a conjunction. It has no bearing on the cases of the nouns and pronouns. It is simply there to connect the stuff before the comma to the stuff after the comma.

While I don't officially cover conjunctions in this book, I think it is important to understand these nuances when talking about certain prepositions. If you want to learn about conjunctions, they are covered in great detail in my A2 German book called "Elementary German with Herr Antrim".

The preposition "wegen" means "because of". You use it in a very similar way in English.

**Wegen der Bedrohung ist diese Straße abgeriegelt. -
Because of the threat, this street is cordoned off.**

**Wegen der Inflation kostet mein Kaffee 5€. -
Because of inflation my coffee costs €5.**

**Fred darf wegen seines Hausarrests
nicht mitkommen. -
Fred can't come along, because of his grounding
(because he was grounded).**

I love that the German word for "being grounded" is "Hausarrest". It just makes me smile.

If you mean to say "because" followed by a phrase you probably need to use the conjunction "weil", "denn" or "da" instead of the preposition "wegen".

Ich kann mir keinen Kaffee leisten, weil die Inflation des Euros steigt. - I cannot afford a coffee because the inflation of the Euro is rising.

Ich kann mir keinen Kaffee leisten, denn die Inflation des Euros steigt. - I cannot afford a coffee because the inflation of the Euro is rising.

Da die Inflation des Euros steigt, kann ich mir keinen Kaffee leisten. - Because the inflation of the Euro is rising, I cannot afford a coffee.

Just remember that when you say "because of" followed by a noun, you need to use the preposition "wegen" and when you follow it with a clause, you need a conjunction like "weil", "denn" or "da".

Now is probably an opportune time to mention that you will often hear the genitive prepositions used with the dative case instead of the genitive. This is almost exclusively in spoken German and is more prevalent in certain regions than in others.

In my mind, it is better to use the genitive case than the dative, as this is what the official guardians of German grammar dogma have said it should be. Just know that you might hear someone say "wegen seinem Hausarrest" instead of "wegen seines Hausarrests".

Also, some people get pretty heated in this debate, so the next time you see an online debate about "wegen + genitive" vs "wegen + dative" tell them this is the only way to do it and anyone using anything other than the genitive case is wrong.

The four (5 if you count "anstelle", 6 if you count "anstatt" and "statt" separately) prepositions I have shown you so far are usually the only ones in textbooks. This is partly because they are the most used ones, but it is also partly because there are easier ways to phrase almost all of the other genitive prepositions.

Rather than teaching these prepositions in lower level courses, teachers and textbook creators will opt to leave them for a much later B1/B2 level lesson. I like to be thorough, so I'm going to teach them to you today anyway.

German	English	German	English
innerhalb	inside of	anlässlich	on the occasion of
außerhalb	outside of	kraft	by virtue of
oberhalb	above	laut	according to
unterhalb	under	aufgrund	on the basis of, because of
diesseits	this side of	seitens	on the part of
jenseits	on the other side of	bezüglich	with regards to

As you can see from the list, lots of these have something to do with the location of something in relation to "this side" vs "that side". Let's start with "innerhalb".

Gegenseitiger Respekt ist äußerst wichtig innerhalb eines Geschäfts. - Mutual respect is crucial inside of a business.

Innerhalb einer Stunde wurde er verhaftet. - Inside of an hour he was arrested.

Rauchen ist innerhalb des Gebäudes verboten. - Smoking is forbidden inside of the building.

The main question you should be asking yourself is "what is the difference between 'in' and 'innerhalb'?" The answer is "not much". This is why most people just use "in" and forget that "innerhalb" exists. To my ear, "innerhalb" sounds more formal.

If you switched all of the examples I just gave and used "in" instead, they would all work. The only one that would have a significant difference is the one that says "innerhalb einer Stunde". The use of "innerhalb" here gives the impression that it was slightly less than one hour. If you use "in", I would think it was scheduled for an hour from some designated time.

If there is an "innerhalb" there must be an "außerhalb". It is the same thing, but the opposite. It means "outside of". You can use it like this.

Außerhalb des Gebäudes sollte man
auch nicht rauchen. -
You shouldn't smoke outside of the building either.

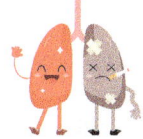

Die Polizei hat sein Auto
außerhalb der Stadt gefunden. -
The police found his car outside of the city.

Warum ist die Milch immer noch
außerhalb des Kühlschranks? -
Why is the milk still outside of the refrigerator?

You can actually use "innerhalb" in all of these examples where "außerhalb" is written and it would make sense. It would just change the location of the thing. I would argue that "außerhalb" is slightly more useful than "innerhalb", as there is no good replacement for "außerhalb". Using "aus" would not have the same meaning, as that would describe the movement out of the thing. "Außerhalb" is used to describe the location of something after it has been moved "aus".

Our next grouping is "oberhalb" (above) and "unterhalb" (under). While you could replace these with "über" and "unter" respectively, the genitive ones feel like they add more distance between the things described. It adds something more grandiose about it all.

Die Sommerrodelbahn liegt
auf dem Berg oberhalb der Stadt. -
The summer toboggan run is located
on the mountain above the city.

Der Clown jongliert **Bälle**
auf einem Hochseil oberhalb des Publikums. -
The clown is juggling balls on a tightrope
above the audience.

Die Sommerrodelbahn ist **auf einem Berg**
oberhalb der Stadt. -
The alpine coaster is on a mountain
above the city.

In these examples, I would only use "über" in one of them. The one with the clown doesn't seem large enough to really need "oberhalb". For the other two examples, I can't think of a better way to say this expression without using "oberhalb".

Der Räuber grub **unterhalb der Bank**. -
The robber dug under the bank.

Manche Flüsse fließen **unterhalb der Erde**. -
Some rivers flow underground.

Die Stadt liegt **unterhalb des Skiurlaubsorts**. -
The city is located below the ski resort.

I would argue for these three examples, the first two sound perfectly fine with "unter", but the last one needs "unterhalb".

The difference between these genitive prepositions and their counterparts is mostly a feeling. It could also be said that the genitive ones sound more formal or stilted, as "über" and "unter" are much more commonly used.

Next up we have the difference between "diesseits" (this side of) and "jenseits" (the other side of). Basically these boil down to "here" and "there". There is some sort of imaginary line. On one side we have "diesseits" and on the other we have "jenseits".

**Dieses Restaurant hat
das beste Barbecue diesseits des Mississippis. -
This restaurant has
the best barbecue this side of the Mississippi.**

**Diesseits der Grenze findet man
viel mehr wilde Blumen. -
On this side of the border you find
many more wild flowers.**

**Diesseits der Grenze ist Marihuana illegal. -
On this side of the border, marijuana is illegal.**

In these examples the speaker is on the same side as the prepositional phrase using "diesseits".

**Jenseits der Grenze kann man es legal kaufen. -
On the other side of the border one can buy it legally.**

**Es gibt viele Obdachlose,
die jenseits dieses Gebäudes leben. -
There are a lot of homeless people
who live on the other side of this building.**

**Jenseits der Brücke steht ein Troll. -
On the other side of the bridge stands a troll.**

In these examples the speakers is not on the same side of the imaginary border as the preposition "jenseits".

Next up we have "seitens". It translates as "on the side of". Unlike the others that I have listed so far, there is no opposite preposition. This is due to the fact that "seitens" changes sides to whichever side shows up after it. Let's see some examples so you know what I mean.

**Die Firma musste wegen Diebstahls
seitens der Arbeitnehmer Bankrott anmelden. -
The company had to declare bankruptcy
because of theft on the part of the employees.**

There are two different genitive prepositions in this sentence. The first is "wegen", which doesn't need an article. Even though the article is missing, we still add -s to the end of the noun, because it is masculine. Due to many people using the dative case with "wegen", you will often find "wegen Diebstahl" written online.

The preposition we are actually here to observe is "seitens". It is followed by a plural nouns, which is why we used the article "der". Together with the previous prepositional phrase, we know who is doing the theft. It is on the side of the employees, which is why they are listed after the preposition "seitens".

**Die Gefährlichkeit des Weges
erfordert Vorsicht seitens der Wanderer. -
The danger of the path requires
caution on the side of the hikers.**

This example uses two genitive objects, too. This time we have a simple possessive usage at the beginning of the sentence to show where the danger lies. The preposition "seitens" is here to tell us who should have "Vorsicht". It should be on the side of the hikers. Again, a plural noun will use the article "der" in the genitive case.

**Es gab eine große Demonstration
seitens der Opposition. -
There was a large demonstration
on the part/side of the opposition.**

The people doing the demonstration in this sentence are on the side of the opposition, which is why "der Opposition" is listed after the preposition, "seitens".

The preposition "anlässlich" is similar to the English "on the occasion of". It sounds a bit elevated and is not very common in everyday speech, but when it is used, it requires the genitive case after it.

**Anlässlich seines hundertsten Geburtstags
flog er nach Las Vegas. -
On the occasion of his 100th birthday,
he flew to Las Vegas.**

128

Here we have an example using "anlässlich" with a birthday. That is a masculine noun, so the article and the noun end with -s. In normal conversation, I would probably just use the preposition "für" instead of "anlässlich" in this sentence.

Meine Frau hat mir ein Buch über Goethe anlässlich unserer silbernen Hochzeit gekauft. - My wife bought me a book about Goethe on the occasion of our silver wedding anniversary.

Again, I would probably use "für" in a real conversation, but this is another example of how to use "anlässlich". It names a special occasion and the rest of the sentence tells what was done for that occasion.

Seine ganze Familie jubelte anlässlich seines Freispruchs. - His entire family cheered on the occasion of his acquittal.

This might be the only example where I might use "anlässlich". I definitely wouldn't use "für" in this sentence, as it doesn't make sense. The preposition "nach" might work better. You could also phrase it with a secondary clause like "als er freigesprochen wurde" (when he was acquitted).

Next up we have "kraft". You may already know this word as a noun "die Kraft" (strength, power). This is the same use here, but we are putting it in front of the thing that grants or creates the power. It's used similarly to the phrase "by the power vested in me", indicating the source of authority.

Der Lehrer darf Weisungen kraft seiner Autorität ausgeben. - The teacher is allowed to give orders by virtue of his authority.

Kraft des Gesetzes sollten wir nicht ohne Grund ins Gefängnis. - By virtue of the law, we shouldn't go to jail without a cause.

Kraft des Gesetzes darf man einen Führerschein anstatt eines Reisepasses als Ausweis benutzen, wenn man innerhalb der USA fliegt. - By law you are allowed to use a driver's license instead of a passport as identification when you are flying inside of the USA.

This is just a gentle reminder that there are a lot of genitive prepositions and there is no rule that says you can't use a bunch of them in the same sentence. Also, this is a real law in the USA that allows you to use a driver's license to identify yourself before a flight within the USA.

As an adjective "laut" means "loud". As a preposition, it most closely resembles "according to". You can use it like this.

Laut des Wetterberichts sollte es morgen regnen. - According to the weather forecast, it is supposed to rain tomorrow.

Laut dieser Zeitung ist der Musiker bei einem Autounfall gestorben. - According to this newspaper the musician died in a car accident.

Laut seines Vaters ist er nicht zu Hause. - According to his father, he isn't at home.

The preposition "aufgrund" literally means "on the grounds of". It generally translates to "because of". While there are several other words you could use to say the same thing, variety is the spice of life, so sprinkle these little words wherever you can.

Flamingos sind aufgrund ihrer Nahrung pink. - Flamingos are pink because of their food.

In case you didn't know, this is a real thing. Flamingos are pink, because they eat algae, brine shrimp, and brine fly larvae in wetlands that all contain carotenoids, which are red-orange pigments. They are actually born grey. I know you didn't come here to learn about flamingos, but that is too cool not to share.

Aufgrund seiner Vorbestrafung hat er den Job nicht bekommen. - Because of his criminal record he didn't get the job.

More true statements. It is quite common for people with criminal records to have difficulty finding jobs. There are even organizations dedicated to finding them jobs or providing places to which they can apply.

Wir haben heute schulfrei aufgrund des Schnees. - We don't have school today because of the snow.

This one might be the least true one for this preposition. It is becoming increasingly common post-COVID to just have e-learning days instead of a traditional snow day. I think we are short changing an entire generation by doing this, but I might be biased, as I get the day off of work, if there is a snow day.

The last genitive preposition I want to talk about is "bezüglich". This translates to "with regards to". It is rooted in the verb "ziehen", which means "to pull". It is like being drawn from the object of the preposition.

Der Bewerber hat ein paar Fragen bezüglich des Vorstellungsgesprächs. - The applicant has a few questions with regards to the interview.

The interview is pulling the questions. In other words, it is the thing that drives the questions to be asked. The questions are "with regards to the interview".

Ich habe eine Frage bezüglich meiner Bewerbung. - I have a question with regard to my application.

The feminine noun requires an -r at the end of the article before it. The question is related to the application, so we used the preposition "bezüglich" to refer to that.

Mein Chef will mit mir
bezüglich meiner Pünktlichkeit sprechen. -
My boss would like to speak to me
regarding my punctuality.

This will not be a good conversation with your boss. No one ever calls you in to a meeting to discuss your punctuality, if it is a good thing. Really this is a meeting about your lack of punctuality. Oh... right. The German stuff. It used the genitive case with a feminine noun. See it? Well, it is the same as all of the other examples.

The bottom line when it comes to the genitive prepositions is the same as the other prepositions. Use the genitive case with genitive prepositions. Use the dative case with the dative ones and the accusative case with the accusative ones.

When it comes to the more obscure prepositions in the genitive list, you can probably get most of the way through B1 or B2 without needing most of them. If you stick to the main four or five I mentioned at the beginning of this section, you will do just fine.

You are now ready to complete exercises 5.7 - 5.9 in the workbook.

Genitive Case Review

To round out this chapter, the genitive case is primarily used for possession. It shows that one noun has ownership or possession of another. In addition to this, it is used for indefinite expressions of time, certain genitive phrases and is required with certain genitive verbs. There are also a variety of genitive prepositions. The genitive case is characterized by articles that end with -s for masculine and neuter nouns and -r for feminine and plural.

To practice everything you learned in this chapter (except genitive verbs, because who needs that noise), complete the exercises in chapter 5 in the workbook or visit the link below.

Extra materials for this chapter:
https://www.germanwithantrim.com/mastering-cases/

Miscellaneous Odds and Ends

Now that we have the topics that are specific to each of the cases out of the way, we can talk about the things that are used across several or all of the cases. Because these topics vary so widely, I would like to remind you to do the worksheets that go with each section before moving on to the next section. This will help you understand each topic individually and keep the ideas separate.

Weak Nouns

The first of such topics is the idea of weak nouns. These are basically nouns that require an extra -n or -en at the end of them when they aren't the subject of the sentence. In other words, they throw a fit, because they aren't the center of attention. This "fit" manifests in the form of some extra letters here and there.

The nouns that do this are all masculine, because of course the masculine ones are the dramatic ones. They were the only ones to go through any changes in the accusative case, if you recall. Many of them end with -e, but that is not a requirement. Here are some general rules that will help you identify them with more ease.

- Masculine nouns that end with -e and are usually people or animals: Neffe (nephew), Junge (boy), Franzose (Frenchman), Hase (hare), Affe (ape).

- Lots of nouns with Latin or Greek endings such as: -ent (Assistent), -ant (Emigrant), -ist (Kapitalist), -at (Diplomat), -aut (Astronaut), -ad (Kamerad).

- A few single syllable masculine nouns: Bär (bear), Christ (Christ), Mensch (person), Prinz (prince), Narr (fool).

Below is a list of some of the more common weak nouns in the nominative and accusative case forms.

der Neffe den Neffen	der Name den Namen	der Held den Helden	der Fels den Felsen
der Kunde den Kunden	der Russe den Russen	der Deutsche den Deutschen	der Löwe den Löwen
der Bauer den Bauern	der Bär den Bären	der Nachbar den Nachbarn	der Idiot den Idioten
der Architekt den Architekten	der Elefant den Elefanten	der Herr den Herrn	

Now let's take a look at a few examples to see what these words look like in action.

Sein Name ist cool. - His name is cool.
Ich mag seinen Namen. - I like his name.

Normally the word "Name" ends with -e, but when it is no longer the subject, it goes from "sein Name" to "seinen Namen". Both the article and the noun get an -n at the end of them.

Der Bär ist in dem Wald. -
The bear is in the forest.
Der Jäger schießt den Bären. -
The hunter shoots the bear.

Some nouns require -en instead of just -n. "Der Bär" is one such noun. While it is not uncommon for nouns that end with consonants to add an -n, this particular example adds -en.

Der Elefant begrüßt den Löwen. -
The elephant greets the lion.
Der Löwe beißt den Elefanten. -
The lion bites the elephant.

This set of examples gives you two nouns for the price of one. When the elephant is the subject, he is content and remains "der Elefant". When he is bitten by the lion, however, he becomes angry and requires extra care in the form of -en at the end of his spelling. The same happens with the lion, but since it already ends with -e, we simply add -n when we get to the accusative case.

Ich gehe heute mit meinem Neffen ins Kino. -
I am going to the movie theater
with my nephew today.

To show you that it isn't reserved for the accusative case, here is an example using "Neffe" in the dative case. The preposition "mit" requires the dative case for whatever noun or pronoun that follows it, which is why we need "meinem Neffen" in this example.

**Außer dem Namen haben wir nichts gemeinsam. -
Besides the name we have nothing in common.**

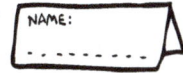

The preposition "außer" also requires the dative case. This changes "der Name" to "dem Namen".

**Der Zoowärter gibt dem Löwen das Steak. -
The zookeeper gives the lion the steak.**

Here the lion is the indirect object (receiving the direct object, steak), which makes him dative. In the dative case we change "der Löwe" into "dem Löwen".

**Du solltest Deutsch mit einem Deutschen üben. -
You should practice German with a German.**

A category that was listed in the rules at the beginning of this chapter is "people". More specifically, however, it often refers to people of a certain origin or nationality. Many times the word for a person from a particular place simply takes the word for the country or language and adds an -e to the end of it to form the masculine noun. This is due to the nouns actually being adjectives in disguise. It is essentially a shortening of the phrase "der deutsche Mann". In the accusative case, it would be "den deutschen Mann".

Some shenanigans happen when we get to the genitive case. Some of the nouns don't get an -s anymore in the genitive case, while others will. Sometimes you just get -n or -en and other times you get that plus -s.

**Der Hund meines Neffen heißt Struppi. -
My nephew's dog is called Struppi.**

The word "Neffe" doesn't get an -s. It replaces the -s that would be at the end of the genitive form with the extra -n.

**Die Bekanntheit seines Namens
ist seine Superkraft. -
The prominence of his name is his superpower.**

The word "Name" by contrast gets both an -n and an -s. If you are hoping I'm going to teach you some sort of trick to know if a noun gets the -s or -es or not, the answer will disappoint you. There is no good way to tell. I often have to look up words on Duden just to make sure I get them right. It is something that comes with exposure, but due to the rare use of the genitive case in conversation, the exposure may take a long time to make its home in your brain.

Der echte Name des Helden ist nicht bekannt. -
The real name of the hero is not known.

Der Rüssel des Elefanten ist sehr lang. -
The trunk of the elephant is very long.

Neither "Held" nor "Elefant" require the -s to be added in the genitive case. It is just another quirk of the genitive case and, more broadly, of the German language.

Complete exercise 6.1 in the workbook before continuing.

Demonstrative and Relative Pronouns

Demonstrative and relative pronouns are basically the same things. The difference is the kinds of sentences they are used in. Both sets of pronouns translate roughly to "that" or some variation thereof in English.

While demonstrative pronouns are generally used in their own sentences, relative pronouns are used to start relative clauses. These are partial sentences attached to the main sentence that describe something from the main sentence in more detail. I know that sounds wordy, but it will make more sense with examples.

Demonstrative and relative pronouns look almost identical to the definite articles. The differences occur in the dative plural form, which is "denen" instead of "den" and all of the genitive pronouns add -en to the end of the original articles. In the case of "des", it also doubles the -s at the end.

The full chart of demonstrative/relative pronouns can be seen on the next page.

	Masculine	Feminine	Neuter	Plural
Nominative	der	die	das	die
Accusative	den	die	das	die
Dative	dem	der	dem	denen
Genitive	dessen	deren	dessen	deren

Siehst du den Tisch da drüben? Der ist sehr teuer. - Do you see the table over there? It is very expensive.

In this example we start with identifying the noun to which the demonstrative pronoun in the next sentence refers. The table is masculine, which means we have to have a masculine demonstrative pronoun. Since it is the subject of the second sentence, I used "der".

Why not just use "er" instead of "der"? It is mostly just a personal preference, but the demonstrative pronoun version puts a bit more emphasis on the word and draws more attention to it. It's like saying "That thing is expensive."

Ich mag diese Hose. Die ist nicht zu eng. - I like these jeans (singular). They aren't too tight.

This sentence follows the same pattern, but uses the feminine pronoun "die" instead. Again, the demonstrative pronoun is the subject, so it is in the nominative case.

Er sucht das Messer. Das ist auf dem Tisch. - He is looking for the knife. It is on the table.

In this sentence we used the neuter noun "Messer", which means we have to use the neuter pronoun "das". This is also a kind of placeholder pronoun. You saw this earlier in sentences like "Wer ist das?" We don't know the gender of the person, so we need to use the gender neutral pronoun.

The same is true of "Was ist das?" The answers also used the placeholder pronoun "das", but this is due to the fact that it doesn't matter rather than not knowing the gender.

**Wir mögen diese Pfirsiche. Die sind lecker. -
We like these peaches. They are delicious.**

In this example we used the plural version of "peach", "Pfirsiche". Therefore we need the plural pronoun "die".

These examples are overly simplistic, but I hope you get the general idea. Demonstrative pronouns are not as widely used as relative pronouns, which is why I will focus on them for the rest of this chapter. Just keep in mind that the rules I explain for relative pronouns also apply for demonstrative pronouns. If the demonstrative pronoun is used in the dative case, it needs to have a dative form.

One other thing to note about the demonstrative pronouns is that they generally show up at the beginning of their sentence. This happens regardless of whether or not they are the subject. This allows us to start the sentence with something like "dem".

When it comes to relative pronouns, you need to keep the following rules in mind.

- The relative pronoun must match the gender of the noun to which it refers. (Masculine nouns require masculine pronouns, feminine-feminine, etc.)
- The relative pronoun will use the grammatical case in which it is used within its own clause regardless of how it is used in the main clause. (If the relative pronoun is the indirect object in the relative clause, use the dative case. If it is the subject of the clause, use the nominative case.)
- The conjugated verb in the relative clause will appear at the end of the clause. (You may be used to this from subordinate clauses. Put all of the other elements in their usual place throughout the clause. Then put the conjugated verb at the end.)

**Siehst du den Tisch, der da drüben steht? -
Do you see the table that is standing over there?**

This example is a version of the first one I wrote with the demonstrative pronouns. It starts with the same statement "Siehst du den Tisch?" The relative clause gives us more context about the table in the question. It tells us which table we mean, the one over there. To be fair, in normal conversation, I would actually say "Siehst du den Tisch da drüben?" and simplify this whole thing, but this is a simple example to show you how things work.

The conjugated verb is at the end of the relative clause. If you are familiar with subordinate clauses, this will make sense. If not, just know that it is exactly that simple. The conjugated verb is at the end of the relative clause. Everything else is in the same spot it always is.

A relative clause must start with a relative pronoun. This means that the only place we can put "der" is directly after the comma.

Ich mag die Hose, die in diesem Bild sind. -
I like the jeans that are in this picture.

In this sentence we used the same logic. The relative pronoun "die" refers back to the feminine noun "die Hose" and give us more context about it. Since "die" is the subject of that clause, it is in the nominative case.

Er sucht das Messer, das auf dem Tisch ist. -
He is looking for the knife, that is on the table.

This sentence does exactly the same thing. In the first half, we introduce the noun to which "das" refers. Then, in the second half, we give more context about the knife through the relative clause. Again, the subject is the relative pronoun, so it is in the nominative case.

Wir mögen diese Pfirsiche,
die vom Bauern kommen. -
We like these peaches, that come from the farmer.

To make sure we have at least one example of every relative pronoun on the list, here is an example that uses a plural noun. This plural noun is then represented again by the relative pronoun "die" at the beginning of the relative clause.

Ich sehe den selben Film, den dieser Man sieht. -
I am watching the same film,
that this man is watching.

139

This is the first of several accusative examples. This shows the direct object of the relative clause as "den", which refers back to the film. Because "dieser Mann" is the one seeing something in the second half of the sentence and we know that the thing he is seeing is the film, we have to use the relative pronoun "den" to indicate the masculine accusative form.

Ich weiß die Antwort, die diese Frau weiß. -
I know the answer, that this woman knows.

While in this sentence it doesn't really matter that the relative pronoun is accusative, because it is feminine, which does not change in the accusative case, I still want to point out that it is the direct object, which is indeed accusative.

Dieses Mädchen, das ich mag,
lässt dieses Buch zu Hause. -
This girl, that I like, leaves this book at home.

This sentence is also using a relative pronoun in the accusative case, but I think it is more important that it points out where relative pronouns can be used and how they work. The relative clause is in the middle of the sentence this time instead of at the very end. This means you can embed the entire clause in the middle and just separate it out with commas. This is exactly what happens in English, too.

Technically speaking you can put a relative clause after any noun you mention anywhere in the sentence. I'm trying to keep my examples relative simple for the purposes of this lesson, but it can get quite complicated, if the writer/speaker wants to make it that way.

Diese Pfirsiche, die ich gekauft habe,
kommen vom Bauern. -
These peaches that I bought come from the farmer.

This example uses the relative clause to describe the subject of the main clause. It interrupts the entire sentence to add this context. Then the rest of the main clause continues after the relative clause. The conjugated verb of the relative clause appears at the end after the past participle, "gekauft".

Mein Bruder, **dem ich** gestern eine E-Mail **geschickt habe,**
hat meine E-Mail **noch nicht beantwortet. -**
My brother, **whom I** sent an email yesterday,
has not yet answered my email.

This sentence kind of implies that you have more than one brother, as the relative clause gives extra details to tell us which brother we mean. In the relative clause, "ich" is the subject and is sending "eine E-Mail" to the brother. This means the brother is the indirect object of the relative clause. This means we need the dative case pronoun "dem" to represent the masculine noun "Bruder".

Er trifft morgen die Frau,
der er sein Auto **verkauft. -**
Tomorrow he **is meeting** the woman,
(to**)** whom he **is selling** his car.

This relative clause describes the direct object "die Frau". In the relative clause, the woman is the indirect object, which again requires the dative case. The feminine relative pronoun in the dative case is "der".

Das Pferd, **dem ich** das Heu **bringe,**
läuft zu mir **rüber. -**
The horse that I **am bringing**
the hay **is running** to me.

Here we have another indirect object within the relative clause. The relative pronoun refers to a neuter noun this time, so I used the pronoun "dem".

Die Kinder, **denen wir** jeden Tag Essen **kochen,**
möchten das Geschirr **nicht spülen. -**
The children that we **cook** food every day
don't want to wash the dishes.

This is the first example that uses a relative pronoun that is not the same as the definite article that we would use in the same situation. If we remove this relative clause and rewrite it as its own sentence, it would look like this.

Wir kochen den Kindern jeden Tag Essen. -
We **cook** the children food every day.

In this version of the sentence we can see the plural dative article "den" in front of the children. When this sentence becomes a relative clause, however, the relative pronoun is "denen", which is what you see in the full sentence above.

Sometimes it is helpful to envision the relative clause as it would have been in a full sentence, so you can better understand the cases that are used within the sentence. This allows you to use the word order rules to help identify the cases.

> **Der Junge, dessen Haare blau sind, spielt den ganzen Tag Computerspiele. - The boy, whose hair is blue, plays computer games the entire day.**

When you use the genitive case relative pronouns, you have to follow them up with whatever noun is being possessed. In this example, the boy is the one that has something. This means that we need the masculine genitive pronoun, "dessen". The word "Haare" is plural, but this does not have any bearing on which relative pronoun we use. The only part that matters is "what is the gender of the person possessing something within the relative clause".

> **Die Frau, deren Mann gestorben ist, hat heute viel zu tun. - The woman, whose husband died, has a lot to do today.**

Here we have a feminine genitive pronoun. The woman is the one who has something. This means we have to use the feminine pronoun even though the thing she has is a masculine noun.

> **Der Polizist fährt mit dem Mädchen, dessen Eltern verschwunden sind, zur Polizeiwache. - The police officer drives with the girl, whose parents disappeared, to the police station.**

In the previous two examples, the relative clause was describing the subject of the main sentence. This sentence uses the relative clause after the end of a prepositional phrase, which uses the dative case. The girl is the one who has the parents mentioned in the relative clause. This means we need the neuter relative pronoun to represent her.

**Die Kinder, deren Schokolade schon gegessen wurde,
wissen nicht, wer sie gegessen hat. -
The children, whose chocolate has already been eaten,
don't know who ate it.**

In our final example we have a plural noun, "Kinder", described in more detail through the genitive case in the relative clause. This means we use the plural genitive pronoun, "deren" to show who has the chocolate.

Relative Pronouns Sidenote

Since question words are technically pronouns, they can be used as relative pronouns, if the information to which you are referring with the relative pronoun is not known or abstract. In those instances, you use the most appropriate question word in place of the relative pronoun.

**Wer ein Stück Kuchen will, muss sich melden. -
Whoever wants a piece of cake, has to raise their hand.**

In this example we are asking a question within the relative clause. Since we are asking for the subject of that clause, we need the nominative case question word "wer". If you simply wrote a question, you would say "Wer will ein Stück Kuchen?" (Who wants a piece of cake?)

**Wen dieses Buch nicht interessiert,
dem ist nicht zu helfen. -
Whomever this book doesn't interest,
they are beyond help.**

In this example we have the accusative case being used as the question word, as "dieses Buch" is the subject of the clause. The book interests someone, but this person is not known, so we used the accusative question word "wer" instead of a normal pronoun. Ironically, we also use a relative pronoun after the comma in the dative case due to the dative verb "helfen".

**Wem Avengers nicht gefällt,
der geht fast nie ins Kino. -
Whomever isn't pleased by Avengers,
almost never goes to the movie theater.**

I used the dative verb "gefallen" in the first clause, which is why our object "wem" has to be shown in the dative case. Since we don't know who this person is (after all, a person who doesn't like Avengers films is pretty rare), we have to use a question word instead of a personal pronoun.

Wessen Katze sie ist, bleibt ungewiss. -
Whose cat it is, remains uncertain.

It is also possible to use this kind of construction with the genitive case. In this example you see exactly that. The cat is the subject of that clause, but it is possessed by some person, which is represented by the question word "wessen", because we don't know this person.

In all of the examples I shows you here you can see a pattern. The first clause is written with a question word at the beginning of it. The second clause expands on the information in the first clause. In the first and last examples, the first clause acts as a sort of subject for the second clause, which is why there is no nominative case noun or pronoun in the second clause.

In the middle two examples, you can see the clause represented again with a demonstrative pronoun to replace it. In the one about a book, the first clause is represented by a dative relative pronoun, "dem". In the one about Avengers, the relative pronoun is in the nominative case, as it is the subject of the second clause. The relative pronoun refers back to the person referenced in the first clause.

In the end, relative pronouns are used to say "that" and give more context to the noun named directly before it. These are used within relative clauses, which require the verb to be at the end of the clause. Since question words aer a kind of pronoun, they can also be used as relative pronouns. Just make sure to use the right case with them.

Complete exercises 6.2 - 6.7 in the workbook before continuing.

Reflexive Pronouns

Reflexive pronouns are words used in place of a noun as the object of a sentence when both the subject and the object are the same person, place or thing. Most of the time, these are used with people, but it is possible to use them in other circumstances. In German, they very closely resemble the personal pronouns in the accusative and dative cases with some exceptions.

The difference occurs in the third person singular (er, sie, es) forms. Instead of each of these words getting their own unique pronoun, as they did for the personal pronouns, reflexive pronouns in the third person use "sich" for every form, accusative and dative. You can see this in the full reflexive pronoun chart below.

Nom	Acc	Dat	Nom	Acc	Dat
ich	mich	mir	wir	uns	uns
du	dich	dir	ihr	euch	euch
er, sie, es	sich	sich	sie, Sie	sich	sich

First let's look at an example of a reflexive pronoun in use, so we understand why we need them.

Er rasiert sich. -
He shaves himself.

This is a pretty basic example. There is a subject, "er", and an object "sich". The subject is shaving the object and the subject and object are the same person.

Ok, but why can't we just say "He shaves." like we would in English? Why do we need to identify the person or thing being shaven?

The verb "rasieren" requires an object. You can't just shave in German. You have to identify the person or object that is being shaven. It's just how the verb works.

Er rasiert sein Gesicht. -
He shaves his face.

So why can't we just say it like this example shows? Wouldn't that be word for word the same sentence in both languages? Yes. It would be, but it doesn't quite work.

The problem here is that we can't be 100% sure that the "er" and "sein" refer to the same person. If you didn't know, it is pretty customary for families to request that someone shave their family members while in a coma, so that they continue to look the way the family remembers them. If the person shaving is masculine and the person being shaven is masculine, the sentence "Er rasiert sein Gesicht." would be used to express this situation.

In order to say "He is shaving his face." and mean that both "he" and "his" refer to the same person, you would need this version of the sentence.

Er rasiert sich das Gesicht. -
He shaves his face.

Why "das Gesicht" and not "sein Gesicht"?

Well, it would be a bit redundant. You already identified whose face it is by using the reflexive "sich". This tells us that the person being shaven is the same "he" as the subject. Once you have done that, you just need to identify the part of that person that is being shaven, which is "das Gesicht".

That said, the sentence "Er rasiert sich sein Gesicht." is a pretty normal way of phrasing this same expression. You can express it either way, but the reflexive pronoun must still be there, no matter which version you use.

Now that you understand the general idea, let's get into a few more examples to help us figure out when to use the accusative case and when to use the dative.

If there is not already a direct object within the sentence and a reflexive pronoun is needed, the reflexive pronoun will be accusative. For example:

Ich ärgere mich über mich. -
I am getting angry (upsetting myself) at myself.

In this sentence "ich" is the subject. This person is also the object of the sentence, which means that we need to represent the same person again. This is a reflexive pronoun. While you can't tell, because the 1st person pronouns are the same as the personal pronouns, we can see the accusative case in action as "mich". The extra accusative case words in this sentence are a preposition and its object.

Freust du dich auf das Wochenende? -
Are you looking (yourself) forward
to the weekend?

This one is a bit tricky, because the English equivalent would not use a reflexive pronoun. In German, however, the verb "freuen" always has a reflexive pronoun nearby. Because of this, we use the accusative pronoun "dich" to represent "du" in the direct object spot. If you want a non-reflexive option, you need "erfreuen".

Er konzentriert sich auf seine Hausaufgaben. -
He is concentrating (himself) on his homework.

This example shows us the first instance of a reflexive pronoun we can readily see. Since the subject is written in the third person (er), the reflexive pronoun must also be used with the third person. Rather than using "ihn" in this sentence, however, which would indicate he is concentrating someone else on his homework (not possible), we used the reflexive pronoun "sich".

Wir interessieren uns für Fußball. -
We are interested (interest ourselves) in soccer.

In yet another example that does not require a reflexive pronoun in English, but does in German, this sentence uses the direct object "uns" as a reflexive pronoun, as the subject is the same group of people (wir).

Entscheidet ihr euch für eine Universität? -
Are you deciding (yourself) for a university?

The verb "entscheiden" also always requires a reflexive pronoun. This time "ihr" is the subject, so we needed the accusative reflexive pronoun "euch".

Sie verlieben sich. -
They are falling in love with each other/themselves.

This sentence is the first example in which we use a reflexive pronoun in both languages. It is more common in English to use the phrasing "with each other" rather than "with themselves", but "each other" still has a similar meaning to the German word "sich" in this example.

The people falling in love and the ones with whom they are falling in love are the same people, so the direct object of the sentence is a reflexive pronoun.

If there is already a direct object in a sentence (usually a body part) with a reflexive pronoun, the reflexive pronoun is in the dative case.

Ich rasiere mich. - I am shaving myself.

**Ich rasiere mir die Beine. -
I am shaving my legs (myself the legs).**

In the first example here, there is no direct object without the reflexive pronoun. This means the reflexive pronoun is the direct object, which requires the accusative case.

In the second example, the legs are already the direct object. In order to still use the reflexive pronoun, we need to put it into the dative case, which is why we used "mir" instead of "mich" in this example.

The deciding factor between accusative and dative reflexive pronouns is the presence of a direct object or the lack thereof. If there is already an object in the sentence before you add in the reflexive pronoun, the reflexive must be dative, as the other object takes the accusative spot. If there is not another object, however, the reflexive pronoun is used in the accusative case.

**Ich putze mir die Zähne. -
I am brushing my teeth.**

This example is similar, as we already have an accusative object, "die Zähne". This forces our reflexive pronoun into the dative case, which is why we used "mir" instead of "mich".

The verb "putzen" can be used to clean a variety of surfaces, which means it is not always used reflexively. In fact, the only way to use "putzen" reflexively is to mean "to brush ones teeth". It is then always paired with the noun "die Zähne".

**Wasch dir die Hände! -
Wash your hands.**

Command form is always confusing for German learners when it comes to reflexive pronouns. How do we know that we need "dir" instead of "euch" or "sich" in this sentence? Where is the subject? It is an implied subject.

The command form for "du" and "ihr" don't retain the pronoun when creating the command. This means that we have two options. It could be "du" or it could be "ihr". Since the verb does not have an ending on it, we know it is the du-form command.

This tells us that we need the reflexive pronoun that matches "du". It is dative, because the hands are already in the direct object spot, so the only one left is the dative spot.

Er kämmt sich die Haare. -
He is combing his hair.

While it doesn't really matter in this sentence, the reflexive pronoun is in the dative case, because "die Haare" are the direct object in the accusative case. The only spot left is the dative case.

Wir rasieren uns die Beine. -
We shave our legs.

Can you see why this one uses the dative reflexive pronoun? Of course, it is because "die Beine" is already taking up the accusative spot, so there wasn't any option left, but the dative case.

Zieht euch die neuen T-Shirts an! -
Put on your new t-shirts.

In this example the new t-shirts are the direct object, which puts the reflexive pronoun into the dative case.

Sie können sich kein neues Auto leisten. -
They can't afford a new car (for themselves).

The verb "leisten" always confused me. I didn't really get how it would be necessary to say "oneself" anywhere in the sentence. How can you afford someone else something? I just couldn't get my brain wrapped around this.

Sometimes it doesn't make much sense. There are just certain verbs that almost always require a reflexive pronoun. While the verb "leisten" does not always require a reflexive pronoun, when it does, it will be used in the dative case, as there will always be some sort of other object within the sentence.

I mentioned earlier that the reflexive pronouns are there to make sure you know that the subject and the object of the sentence are the same person. This, of course, means that you can also use things other than reflexive pronouns with lots of these verbs.

Many German teachers say that these are "reflexive verbs", because they "always" require a reflexive pronoun. This simply isn't true. Real reflexive verbs are incredibly rare. The rest of the "reflexive verbs" can be use non-reflexively.

Let's take a look at a few examples to see what I mean.

**Ich putze meinem Sohn die Zähne. -
I am brushing my son's teeth.**

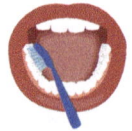

If you have small children, you know that before they become self-sufficient and can brush their own teeth, you have to do it for them. This means, of course, you can say "I am brushing my son's teeth." and it makes perfect sense in both languages.

There is no need for a reflexive pronoun, as the person being brushed is not the same as the person brushing. This means that the dative case object simply identifies the person to whom the teeth belong.

**Er wäscht seiner Tochter die Hände! -
He washes his daughter's hands.**

This one is similar. The daughter cannot (or will not, if your children are stubborn like mine) wash their hands. So he helps her. The sentence structure is the same, but instead of using the reflexive pronoun "sich" as we would when he washes his own hands, we use the dative case "seiner Tochter".

Er kämmt dem Mann die Haare. -
He is combing the man's hair.

The same logic is applied here. The man is not combing his own hair. He is combing another man's hair. Maybe this is a nursing home. Maybe it is a hospital. Maybe it is just a weird guy on the subway, but whatever it is, the man being combed is not the same as the subject, so we don't have a reflexive pronoun.

Traditional reflexive verbs are not the only times that we use phrases like this, however. There are a few times when you will use a dative object even though there is not already an object in the sentence. This happens when you hit someone or tap them on the head or shoulder.

Sie haut ihm auf den Kopf. -
She hits him on the head.

She is the subject of the sentence and is hitting someone else. Because of the way it is phrased, the German language kind of classified this phrase as the same as the ones from the previous page of examples. For that reason, the man is in the dative case. I used a regular personal pronoun here instead of a reflexive pronoun, as he is not her.

Er klopft ihr auf die Schulter. -
He taps her on the shoulder.

The verb "klopfen" usually means "to knock" and is used when you visit someone else's house and their doorbell doesn't work. When used with people, it usually means "to tap", as in "to touch lightly in an attempt to get their attention". This is exactly what happens in this example.

Again, the subject and object are not the same person, so we don't need a reflexive pronoun. We also don't technically have a direct object, so our normal logic would say that we should use "sie" in the accusative case instead of the dative "ihr". That doesn't work, however, as there is a body part involved, so we pretend it counts as the direct object.

151

For the most part, reflexive pronouns are not confusing. They are mostly the same as the personal pronouns with the exception of the third person pronouns. These are all "sich" regardless of their gender or if they are singular or plural. You only use a reflexive pronoun, however, when the subject and direct object are the same person.

Complete exercises 6.8 - 6.16 in the workbook before continuing.

Adjectives

Adjectives are words that describe nouns, meaning they describe people, places, things and ideas. In English, this can be done directly before the noun, which is how you are probably thinking this is done, or it can be done far away from the noun.

When we use the adjective away from the noun, we call it a predicate adjective. The predicate, as I mentioned in a previous chapter, is the part of the sentence after the verb. As the name suggests, these adjectives show up after the verb and describe the noun at the beginning.

In German we have the exact same two options. You can put the adjective directly before the noun or you can put it after the verb to describe the subject. Here are a few examples.

Der Film war gut. - The film was good.
Mein Bruder ist jung. - My brother is young.
Die Kinder sind heute laut. - The children are loud today.

In those sentences, the words "good", "young" and "loud" are adjectives that describe the subjects of "the film", "my brother" and "the children". In German it is exactly the same. The adjectives "gut", "jung" and "laut" describe the subjects "der Film", "mein Bruder" and "die Kinder".

This is the easiest way to use adjectives, but it doesn't lend itself to very much variety or flexibility. That's why there is also the option to put the adjective directly before the noun they describe. This allows us the greatest amount of flexibility with our descriptors.

Let's take a look at some examples to see what this looks like.

Der gute Film beginnt in 30 Minuten. -
The good film starts in 30 minutes.

**Ich mag meinen jüngeren Bruder. -
I like my younger brother.**

**Die Mutter gibt den lauten Kindern keine Schokolade. -
The mother isn't giving
the loud children any chocolate.**

As you can see from these examples, we are no longer limited to describing the subject of the sentence when we add the adjective directly in front of the noun. In fact, we can describe any noun we like within the sentence. The placement of the adjective in German and English is exactly the same, between the article (the word for the, a or an) and the noun.

What you may have noticed, however, is that the endings for the German adjectives changed sometimes. The first one used an -e while the last two used -en. As you probably guessed, this has to do with the gender of nouns and the cases in which they are used.

What you might not have guessed is that it also depends on what comes before the adjective. Definite articles (der-words) require different adjective endings than indefinite articles (ein-words) and there is a third category when there is no article. Let's start with the adjectives after der-words.

Adjectives After Der-Words

In the chart at the top of the next page you can see all of the definite articles for each case and gender. Next to them you can see the endings for the adjectives that follow them.

I included an example noun and adjective together, so you can see the whole picture. Each article is highlighted in the color of the case and the endings added to the adjectives are also highlighted in the same colors.

At first this may seem overwhelming, but there are really only 2 endings. In the nominative case, all of the singular forms require an -e at the end of the adjective. In the accusative case, feminine and neuter nouns require an -e at the end of the adjective. All of the other forms in all of the other cases require -en at the end. This makes this group of adjective endings by far the easiest to remember.

153

	Masculine	Feminine	Neuter	Plural
Nom	der dumme Mann	die kluge Frau	das fleißige Mädchen	die kleinen Kinder
Acc	den dummen Mann	die kluge Frau	das fleißige Mädchen	die kleinen Kinder
Dat	dem dummen Mann	der klugen Frau	dem fleißigen Mädchen	den kleinen Kindern
Gen	des dummen Mannes	der klugen Frau	des fleißigen Mädchens	der kleinen Kinder

If the noun is plural and you are using a definite article, you add -en to the end of the adjective. If the noun is in the dative or genitive case and there is a definite article before the adjective, add -en. If the noun is masculine and in the accusative case, add -en.

When I teach this in my classes I highlight the endings that are simply -e and contrast those with the -en endings. The -e endings line up in the form of Oklahoma (known for its panhandle shape). That means the rest of the stuff in the chart is Texas. I mention that the people of Oklahoma are my Oklahom-E's and the people of Texas are Tex-Ens. This tends to help people remember which endings go where.

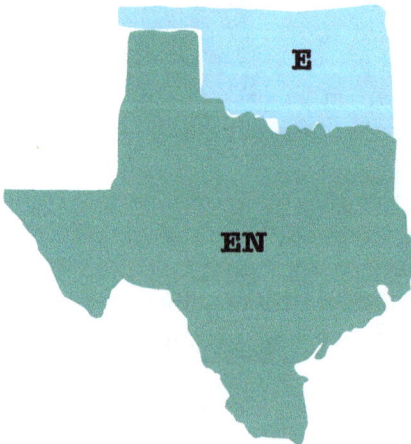

	M	F	N	Pl
Nom	E	E	E	EN
Acc	EN	E	E	EN
Dat	EN	EN	EN	EN
Gen	EN	EN	EN	EN

Don't forget that der-words aren't just der, die, and das. This category includes the additional der-words; dieser, jeder, manche, and so on. This means we can have any of the following examples in the nominative case. And the ending will be the same.

der kleine Mann - **the short man**
dieser kleine Mann - **this short man**
jeder kleine Mann - **every short man**

Dieser hübsche Arzt gibt jedem kranken Patienten solche weißen Zettel. -
This handsome doctor gives every sick patient this kind of white slips of paper.

Here we have several adjectives. The doctor is masculine and the subject of the sentence. This makes him use the nominative case and the der-word ends with -er as a result. The adjective that follows is within Oklahoma on our chart, so it gets an -e.

The word "Zettel" is used in the plural form. So even though it is in the accusative case and the article ends with -e, the adjective gets -en, as it is between an article and a plural noun.

The patient is masculine and receiving the slips of paper. This makes them the indirect object and dative. The masculine article ending for nouns in the dative case is -em, but the adjectives that follow them receive -en. This falls below the southern portion of Oklahoma.

Diese kluge Schülerin sagt dieser weisen Lehrerin jede richtige Antwort. -
This smart student tells this wise teacher every correct answer.

In this sentence, all of the nouns are feminine. In the nominative and accusative cases, this means that both the article and the adjective end with -e. For the indirect object, "Lehrerin", we have to use the dative case, which receives -er for the article ending and -en for the adjective.

Jedes fleißige Mädchen gibt jedem braunen Pferd dieses frische Heu. -
Every hard-working girl gives every brown horse this fresh hay.

Here we have all neuter nouns. The girl and the hay both receive an -es at the end of the article and an -e at the end of the adjective, as they are nominative and accusative. In the dative case, the article gets -em and the adjective that follows gets -en. The girl and the hay are in Oklahoma, while the horse is in Texas.

Diese netten Eltern **zeigen** **allen glücklichen Kindern**
diese neuen Spielzeuge. -
These nice parents **show** **all of the happy children**
these new toys.

All of the nouns in this sentence are plural. Regardless of the case in which it is used, every adjective after a der-word with a plural noun with add -en to the end of the adjective. The nominative and accusative articles get an -e, while the dative article gets -en.

Der Hund **des alten Mannes** **ist braun.** -
The dog **of the old man** **(The old man's** **dog**) **is brown.**

This example includes a genitive noun, "Mann", and an adjective before it. The man is masculine, which gives us the article "des". Since all of the genitive case falls in Texas, we know that the ending on the adjective is -en no matter what.

Die Katze **der netten Frau** **ist grau.** -
The cat **of the nice lady** **(The nice lady's** **cat**) **is grey.**

This is the same idea. Again, the genitive case always requires -en on the adjective regardless of the gender of the noun. The article gets -er, but the adjective after is gets -en.

Das Besteck **des ganzen Publikums** **ist verschwunden.** -
The cutlery **of the entire audience** **has disappeared.**

This example includes a neuter noun in the genitive case, so the article is "des" while the adjective ends with -en.

**Die Nächte der kleinen Städte
sind mir sehr langweilig. -
The nights of the small cities are very boring to me.**

This one gets -en for two reasons. It is both genitive and plural, so the adjective gets -en either way.

Complete exercises 6.17 - 6.19 in the workbook before continuing.

Adjectives After Ein-Words

When you use an indefinite article in German, words that translate as "a" or "an" in English, you mostly use the same endings as you do for definite articles, words that translate as "the" in English.

In fact, all of the dative and genitive adjective endings are still -en. The only change between the adjectives after definite articles chart and the adjectives after indefinite articles chart are with the masculine and neuter forms in the nominative case and the neuter form in the accusative case. These adjectives now require the same letter that would have been on the definite article.

The chart for these endings looks like this.

	Masculine	Feminine	Neuter	Plural
Nom	ein dummer Mann	eine kluge Frau	ein fleißiges Mädchen	meine kleinen Kinder
Acc	einen dummen Mann	eine kluge Frau	ein fleißiges Mädchen	meine kleinen Kinder
Dat	einem dummen Mann	einer klugen Frau	einem fleißigen Mädchen	meinen kleinen Kindern
Gen	eines dummen Mannes	einer klugen Frau	eines fleißigen Mädchens	meiner kleinen Kinder

Again, don't forget that in addition to the ein-words listed on the chart, there are also possessive adjectives and the negative ein-word, "kein", which all take the same endings. This means our examples could look like any of the examples you see on the next page.

ein kleiner Mann - a short man
mein lieber Mann - my dear husband
kein kleiner Mann - no short man

Now let's look at some example sentences to see how one might use these adjective endings in a more practical sense.

Mein jüngster Sohn bringt seinem faulen Opa einen neuen Golfschläger. -
My youngest son brings his lazy grandpa a new golf club.

In this sentence I used three masculine nouns. The first one is "Sohn", which is the subject of the sentence and is represented by the nominative case. Because ein-words do not need endings in the nominative case for masculine nouns, the adjective takes over and shows the gender of the noun with -er at the end. Think of it as the adjective adding the ending that would be on a der-word, because the ein-word does not officially identify the gender.

The direct object is "Golfschläger". This is also a masculine noun and is represented in the accusative case. Every ending for masculine nouns in the accusative case is -en. This is true of der-words, ein-words and even the adjectives that follow them. Even if there is no article at all, the ending on the adjective is still -en. If it is masculine and accusative, add -en wherever you can.

The son is giving the golf club to someone. This someone is the indirect object and therefore uses the dative case. When a masculine noun is used in the dative case, the article gets -em and the adjective that follows uses -en. This part is in Texas on our chart, so we know the adjective ends with -en.

Eine schöne Frau kauft einem hübschen Mann eine große Tasse Tee. -
A beautiful woman is buying a handsome man a large cup of tea.

This sentence starts with a feminine noun in the nominative case. Feminine nouns in the nominative and accusative cases will use -e at the end of everything. This means the article ends with -e and so does the adjective. This is why "eine schöne Frau" and "eine große Tasse Tee" have the same endings for everything. They are both feminine. While one is nominative and the other is accusative, they all require -e.

The indirect object of this sentence is another masculine noun, which is why it requires -em at the end of the article and -en at the end of the adjective, just like the example from our last sentence.

**Mein niedliches Kätzchen bringt
einem sprachlosen Mädchen ein totes Mäuschen. -
My cute kitten brings a speechless girl
a dead mouse.**

In this example there are only neuter nouns. In the nominative and accusative cases, there is no ending on the ein-word. This forces our adjective to show the gender of the noun in a similar way to what happens with masculine nouns in the nominative case. Instead of the masculine ending -er, however, the neuter nouns require the adjective to end with -es. This works for both "mein niedliches Kätzchen" and "ein totes Mäuschen"?

In the dative case, we use the same endings as with masculine nouns. The article gets -em and the adjective gets -en.

**Meine kleinen Kinder kaufen
ihren tollen Eltern keine coolen Geschenke. -
My small children don't buy
their great parents any cool gifts.**

This example uses only plural nouns. The nominative and accusative cases are the same. The article gets -e and the adjective uses -en for their endings. The dative case requires -en at the end of everything. This means that both the article and the adjective (and even the noun most of the time) end with -en.

**Ein Hund eines alten Mannes ist weggelaufen. -
A dog of an old man (An old man's dog) ran away.**

Just as we did with the der-word adjective endings, all of the adjective endings in the genitive case preceded by an ein-word require -en. Just don't forget that masculine and neuter nouns in the genitive case will require -es at the end of the article and -s at the end of the noun. If the noun is only one syllable, like our example "Mann", you will add -es to the noun.

**Ein Zimmer eines verfluchten Hotels ist sehr preiswert. -
A room of a haunted hotel is very inexpensive.**

This example shows the neuter form that matches the same rules we saw in the previous example.

**Eine Katze einer netten Frau frisst mein Frühstück. -
A cat of a nice lady (A nice lady's cat)
is eating my breakfast.**

**Die Blumenblätter meiner schönen Blumen sind rosa. -
The petals of my beautiful flowers are pink.**

In these two examples we see the feminine and plural forms for the genitive case. Both require -er at the end of the article and -en at the end of the adjective. Don't forget there is nothing added to the noun for feminine and plural nouns in the genitive case. We only add -s or -es if the noun is masculine or neuter.

Complete exercises 6.20 - 6.22 in the workbook before continuing.

Unpreceded Adjectives

So far we have two of the three adjective ending categories covered. we have seen the adjective endings after definite and indefinite articles. When neither a definite nor an indefinite article is used, the adjective ending generally follows the ending that is normally on the definite articles. The only exceptions are in the genitive case for masculine or neuter nouns.

In addition to simply having nothing in front of the adjective, there are other words that count as "no article". Those include words like "viel", "etwas", "viele", "wenig", "einig" and any numbers. For example: The chart looks like this.

As I said, these endings are used when there is neither a definite nor indefinite article in front of the adjective. This is pretty rare with singular forms, but it can be done.

On the next page you can see the full chart of endings with example nouns and adjectives.

	Masculine	Feminine	Neuter	Plural
Nom	guter Käse	frische Milch	grünes Obst	kleine Kinder
Acc	guten Käse	frische Milch	grünes Obst	kleine Kinder
Dat	gutem Käse	frischer Milch	grünem Obst	kleinen Kindern
Gen	guten Käses	frischer Milch	grünen Obstes	kleiner Kinder

viel frischer Käse - a lot of fresh cheese
etwas frischer Käse - some fresh cheese
fünf kleine Stücke - five small pieces

Now let's see what these adjective endings might look like in full sentences.

Frischer Käse riecht gut. -
Fresh cheese smells good.

Normally in the nominative case we would say "der Käse", but since we are using an adjective and no article, the -er at the end of "der" goes to the adjective, so we end up with "frischer Käse".

Ich mag frischen Käse. -
I like fresh cheese.

The accusative article would be "den" for a masculine noun, but when there is no article, the adjective gets the same ending, so we say "frischen Käse" in this example.

Ich esse gern Salat mit frischem Käse. -
I like to eat salad with fresh cheese.

161

The dative masculine article is "dem", but when there is no article, the adjective takes on this ending to become "frischem Käse".

Der Geruch frischen Käses gefällt mir. -
I like the smell of fresh cheese.
(The smell of fresh cheese is pleasing to me.)

While the genitive masculine article would have been "des", the gender and case can already be seen through the -s at the end of "Käse", so we do not add -es to the adjective here.

Weiße Milch ist am besten. -
White milk is the best.

Ich mag weiße Milch. -
I like white milk.

In the nominative and accusative cases, the feminine article would be "die", which ends with -e. When there is no article, the adjective takes on this ending and becomes "weiße Milch" in these examples.

Ich backe jeden Tag mit weißer Milch. -
I bake with white milk every day.

Ich mag den Geschmack weißer Milch aber nicht. -
I don't like the taste of white milk, however.

In the dative and genitive cases, the feminine noun requires the article "der". Again, there are no articles in this example, so we use the -er at the end of the adjective instead of the article.

Grünes Gemüse sollte gesund sein. -
Green vegetables are supposed to be healthy.

**Meine Kinder essen täglich grünes Gemüse. -
My children eat green vegetables every day.**

For both nominative and accusative with neuter nouns, we would normally use the article "das". Instead of adding -as to the end of the adjective, we add -es. This is similar enough, however, that it still follows the rules I have shown you so far.

**Wir kochen gerne mit grünem Gemüse. -
We like to cook with green vegetables.**

The dative neuter article would be "dem". We simply put the -em on the adjective and now we have the non-preceded adjective "grünem Gemüse".

**Der Vitamingehalt grünen Gemüses ist sehr hoch. -
The vitamin content of green vegetables is very high.**

Again, the genitive masculine and neuter forms do not follow the same patterns we have seen so far, as the ending on the noun already tells us the gender and case. This means we use -en at the end of the adjective like we would if there were any kind of article in front of the adjective.

**Kleine Kinder lügen oft. -
Little children often lie.**

**Er hat zwei kleine Kinder. -
He has two small children.**

Similar to the feminine nouns, the plural articles for nominative and accusative are "die". We add the -e from this article to the end of the adjective to get "kleine Kinder" in both of these examples. Don't forget that "zwei" describes the children, but does not count as an article, as it is not on the der-word or ein-word lists.

Dieser alte Mann gibt kleinen Kindern Bonbons. -
This old man gives little children candies.

I mentioned before that the dative plural gets -en for everything and this is no exception. Regardless of what kind of article there is or if there is an article at all, everything gets -en for dative plural.

Die Stimmen kleiner Kinder sind erschrecklich,
wenn du alleine bist. -
The voices of little children are terrifying,
if you are alone.

In the genitive case, we use -er at the end of the adjective, as the article would normally be "der", just like it is for the feminine nouns in the genitive case. So we end up with "kleiner Kinder" for our final form.

Now that you know all of the adjective endings based on what kind of article they use, it is time for the overview. Some students don't like seeing three different charts for adjective endings. For this reason, I created the chart below. This chart includes der-words, ein-words and non-preceded adjective endings all in one.

At the bottom of the chart, you can also see the words that count as each category, so you don't get confused by something like "ihr" as a possessive, which counts as an ein-word.

	Masculine	Feminine	Neuter	Plural
Nominative	der + -e ein + -er --- + -er	die + -e eine + -e --- + -e	das + -e ein + -es --- + -es	die + -en (k)eine + -en --- + -e
Accusative	den + -en einen + -en --- + -en	die + -e eine + -e --- + -e	das + -e ein + -es --- + -es	die + -en (k)eine + -en --- + -e
Dative	dem + -en einem + -en --- + -em	der + -en einer + -en --- + -er	dem + -en einem + -en --- + -em	den + -en (k)einen + -en --- + -en
Genitive	des + -en eines + -en --- + -en	der + -en einer + -en --- + -er	des + -en eines + -en --- + -en	der + -en (k)einer + -en --- + -er
Categories	Der-Words: der, die, das, den, dem, des, dieser, jeder, manche, alle, solche, welcher		Ein-Words: ein, kein, mein, dein, sein, ihr, unser, euer, Ihr	Unpreceded: viel, etwas, viele, wenig, einige, #s

164

This chart can be overwhelming for some and for others it is simply too small of a font. For either group of people, all of the charts in this chapter as well as any of the other materials throughout the entire book can be found by using the links throughout the book. This chapter's book is located at the very end of the chapter.

Complete exercises 6.23 - 6.27 in the workbook before continuing.

Verbs with Fixed Prepositions

There is a phenomenon in pretty much every language where certain verbs are combined with certain prepositions. These are often called "verbs with fixed prepositions", although I personally hate this name, as these aren't the only prepositions that can be used with these verbs and sometimes they aren't required at all.

You can also call them "prepositional verbs". The bottom line is that it is very *likely* if you use X verb, you need Y preposition with it.

Sometimes this is done with a preposition that simply uses the same case no matter what. For example:

Er entscheidet sich für die Pizzeria. - He decided (himself) for the pizzeria.

No one cares that "sich entscheiden" is combined with "für". We simply tack on the accusative case behind it and move on with our lives. The preposition "für" always uses the accusative case, so the fact that it is used with this verb is irrelevant.

Wir bitten Sie um Vergebung. - We are asking you for forgiveness.

The verb "bitten" is often paired with the preposition "um". It always uses the accusative case, which is why it isn't that complicated.

Verbs with Fixed Accusative Prepositions

I'm going to ignore most of the combinations of accusative prepositions with verbs and instead concentrate on the verbs that use two-way prepositions, which could use accusative or dative. When they are combined with certain verbs, it is difficult to make a guess as to whether it should use accusative or dative. The verbs in the list on the next page use the accusative case.

denken an - to think of/about
sich freuen auf - to look forward to
warten auf - to wait for
sich erinnern an - to remember
glauben an - to believe in

Here's how you can use these verbs in sentences.

Ich denke an dich. -
I am thinking about you.
(I am casting my thoughts in your direction.)

You are supposed to use the accusative case with the preposition "an", if there is a change in location. There doesn't appear to be a change in location when you are thinking about someone. I could make a stretch and use the logic I wrote in parentheses above. If you are putting your thoughts in the direction of someone, the prepositional phrase with them in it would show a change in location for those thoughts. Admittedly, this is a bit of a stretch.

So if you can't rely on the stretched logic idea, how can you decide if the two-way preposition uses the accusative or dative case with these verbs? Unfortunately, this is one of those things that you just have to memorize. I would say, anytime you see a verb and preposition combination that you don't think fits into the usual "change of location" logic, you have to note that and put it in your memory bank.

Meine Tochter freut sich auf das Wochenende. -
My daughter is looking forward to the weekend.

You can look forward to something with the accusative case and the preposition "auf". You can also combine this verb with the preposition "über" and the accusative case to say you are excited about something. Switch "auf" with "über" in the sentence above and your daughter would be excited about the weekend. The difference is subtle, but big enough that you should know the difference.

Since you have to memorize these verb and preposition pairs, you would think there would be a good centrally located list of all of the preposition and verb combinations, but I haven't found one. So I made my own list. The link is listed at the end of this chapter.

Wartest du auf den Bus? -
Are you waiting for the bus?

How is waiting for something a change in location? No idea. Just know that "auf" uses the accusative case when combined with "warten".

Erinnerst du dich immer noch an dieses Mädchen? -
Do you still remember this girl?

Remembering someone requires the accusative case with the preposition "an".

Ich glaube nicht mehr an den Osterhasen. -
I no longer believe in the Easter Bunny.

Yep. Believing in something uses "an" with the accusative case.

Verbs with Fixed Dative Prepositions

I know this will come as a shock, but there are also times when you will use a preposition with a verb that requires the dative case. For example:

Ein Leben besteht aus vielen kleinen Momenten. -
A life consists of a lot of small moments.

Seine Frau bleibt immer noch bei ihm. -
His wife is still staying with him.

These two examples use prepositions that always use the dative case. That makes them super easy to remember and use. I would argue it also makes them so you don't have to remember them at all. You can just intuitively know that the preposition "aus" goes with the verb "bestehen", when you mean that something "consists of something". You can use "bei" with "bleiben" to mean that a person "stays with another person".

As you likely have guessed, there are times when you will use a two-way preposition with the dative case and it won't make much sense on the surface, just like we did for the accusative case. For example:

Die Zwillinge unterscheiden sich in ihren Eigenarten. -
The twins differ in their mannerisms.

While you could make an argument about the figurative nature of the preposition "in" in this sentence, it really would be a stretch to say there is a location here at all, let alone a static location. This one uses the dative case, because I said so. Just roll with it.

There are a bunch of these combinations that don't make much sense, if you follow the logic about two-way prepositions that I outlined in the chapter about them. You simply have to memorize which verb and preposition pairs require the accusative case and which ones require the dative case.

sich täuschen in - to be wrong about
sich fürchten vor - to be afraid of
schützen vor - to protect from
warnen vor - to warn about

These are a few common combinations you may come across. Each of them use the dative case, but use a two-way preposition. Here are a few more examples that help drive the point home.

Ich habe mich in seiner Ehrlichkeit getäuscht. -
I was mistaken about his honesty.

If you try to stretch the limitations of logic, you might be able to think of this as an answer to the question "Where were you mistaken?" The location of this mistake is "in his honesty". Again, this is a bit of a stretch of the logic, but it is kind of pointing to the location of the mistake.

**Chuck Norris fürchtet sich
vor dem Yeti nicht. -
Chuck Norris isn't afraid of the yeti.**

This one also kind of make sense. If you are afraid of something, you usually don't have that fear everywhere you go. It only shows up when you are in front of (vor) the thing that causes the fear. This is a static location where the fear is taking place, so we used the dative case with "vor".

**Der Regenschirm schützt mich vor dem Regen. -
The umbrella protects me from the rain.**

Similarly, you can use "vor" when being protected from something. If you follow the logic I gave for the previous sentence, the thing that is protecting you is before you. It is in front of you to protect you from the rain.

My English-speaking brain wants to say "von" every time, however, which is why we say it is a verb and preposition combination that you have to memorize.

**Meine Mutter hat mich
vor solchen Männern gewarnt. -
My mother warned me about men like that.**

I don't have a logical argument to make here. I don't know why we use "vor" and I don't know why it uses the dative case. It does both of those things, however. On another note, you could say "such men" instead of "men like that". This would be a more direct translation and make it easier to see the changes between the languages, but it just sounded unnatural to me when I wrote it, so I kept "men like that" in the translation.

Again, the bottom line is that certain prepositions are commonly paired with certain verbs. When the two-way prepositions are used like this, we have to worry about which case to choose for each of them. The only real way to learn them is to memorize them as you encounter them.

You can find a list of as many of these verb-preposition combinations I could think of in this chapter's folder at
https://www.germanwithantrim.com/mastering-cases/

Complete exercises 6.28 - 6.30 in the workbook before continuing.

Prepositional Adjectives

In addition to certain verbs being commonly paired with certain prepositions, there are also prepositions that go well together with certain adjectives. A lot of these adjective and preposition combinations use prepositions that always use a particular case. For example:

wegen etwas angeklagt - accused of something
süchtig nach - addicted to
begeistert von - enthusiastic about
bereit zu - ready for
fähig zu - capable of
überzeugt von - convinced of
verrückt nach - crazy about
bekannt für - famous for

Der Mann wurde wegen Diebstahls angeklagt. - The man was accused of theft.

The preposition "wegen" uses the genitive case, which is why "Diebstahl" has an -s at the end of it.

Herr Antrim ist süchtig nach Keksen. - Herr Antrim is addicted to cookies.

Because the preposition "nach" requires the dative case, the plural form of the noun "Keks", which usually just gains an -e, also gains an -n to match the case.

Sie ist begeistert von ihrem neuen Job. - She is enthusiastic about her new job.

Whenever you see "von", it uses the dative case. That is why we have -em at the end of the possessive article and -en at the end of the adjective.

Sometimes, however, they use a two-way preposition, which, as you probably have already guessed, isn't always so cut and dried. In general, the vast majority of the two-way prepositions used in this way use the accusative case. For example:

böse auf - **angry** at
gespannt auf - **in suspense** about
gewöhnt an - **accustomed** to
neidisch auf - **jealous** of
stolz auf - **proud** of
wütend auf - **furious** at
wütend über - **furious** about

Kain ist böse auf seinen Bruder. -
Cain is angry at his brother.

Two Cain and Able references in one book? You know it is a good book now. Anyway, being angry at someone requires the accusative case with the preposition "auf".

Sabrina ist gespannt auf den neuen Film. -
Sabrina is in suspense about the new movie.

Wir sind an das kalte Wetter gewöhnt. -
We are accustomed to the cold weather.

Maggie ist neidisch auf Jakes Erfolg. -
Maggie is jealous of Jake's success.

Milton ist wütend auf seinen Chef. -
Milton is furious at his boss.

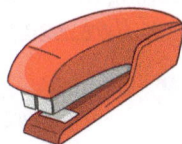

Occasionally they will use the dative case with the two-way preposition. For example:

beteiligt an - **involved in**
interessiert an - **interested in**
sicher vor - **safe from**
gut in - **good at**
blass vor - **pale from**

Er ist an dem Projekt beteiligt. -
He is involved in the project.

Sie ist an Geschichte interessiert. -
She is interested in history.

Wir sind sicher vor dem Sturm. -
We are safe from the storm.

Sie ist gut in Mathematik. -
She is good at math.

Er ist blass vor Angst. -
He is pale from fear.

Since every sentence in this category is pretty much formulated the same way (subject, form of sein, adjective, preposition, noun), I think that is enough examples.

Unfortunately, the German language is full of these kinds of adjective-preposition combinations. You can get a huge list of these combinations by opening this chapter's folder at
https://www.germanwithantrim.com/mastering-cases/

You now have enough information to complete the remaining exercises in the workbook. Exercises 6.31 - 6.33 are all about the adjective-preposition combinations using the list linked above. Exercises in chapter 7 are a general review that incorporate several topics across all of the chapters in this book. It can also be used as a final exam of sorts.

Odds & Ends Review

This chapter is pretty much just a pile of things I didn't think fit anywhere else in the book. They are topics that affect multiple cases or float in that weird limbo between cases. Let's take a trip down memory lane.

Weak Nouns - Nouns that add -n or -en when they aren't the subject (i.e. nominative).

Demonstrative and Relative Pronouns - Basically using der-words as pronouns. While demonstrative pronouns do this in their own sentences, relative pronouns do it to describe a noun in a separate clause. This makes the word order all wonky.

Reflexive Pronouns - The subject and object of the sentence are the same person (usually a person, but not always). There needs to be a reflexive pronoun used. Most of the time they looks just like personal pronouns, but the third person singular (er, sie, es) and plural (sie) pronouns are "sich".

Adjectives - Adjective endings fall into three categories: after der-words, after ein-words and unpreceded. There are lots of -e and -en endings for adjectives after der-words and adjectives after ein-words. The unpreceded category of adjective mostly use the endings from the der-word chart, but the gentive case uses -n where it normally has -s.

Verbs with fixed prepositions - There are certain verbs that are commonly paired with certain prepositions. While most of the time they are easy, because the preposition uses whatever case it normally does, the two-way prepositions make this complicated. It is best to simply memorize which case to use with each preposition and verb combination.

Prepositional Adjectives - Just like verbs with fixed prepositions, these aer adjectives that use certain prepositions. It is often difficult to find the logic in the translation and why you use one preposition over the other. Again, rote memorization is the way to go here.

Extra materials for this chapter:
https://www.germanwithantrim.com/mastering-cases/

From Theory to Practice

As we come to the end of our journey through the German case system, it's essential to reflect on the vast array of topics we've covered. From understanding what grammatical cases are to mastering the intricacies of the nominative, accusative, dative, and genitive cases, you've gained a comprehensive overview of how these elements function individually and together. We've explored the roles of weak nouns, various pronouns, adjectives, and a myriad of prepositions, all of which are crucial for a deeper understanding of German grammar.

To solidify your understanding, I encourage you to apply these principles in real-world contexts. Engage in conversations, write essays, and translate sentences, paying close attention to the grammatical structures. Utilize the additional resources provided, such as flashcards and worksheets, to reinforce your learning.

To make your practice more effective, immerse yourself in the language as much as possible. Watch German movies and TV shows with subtitles to see how native speakers use the case system in everyday conversations. Listen to German podcasts and try to identify the cases being used. This will not only improve your listening skills but also help you internalize the grammatical structures.

Additionally, consider joining a language exchange program or finding a language partner. Conversing with native speakers or fellow learners allows you to use the cases in spontaneous speech, which is invaluable for solidifying your knowledge. Don't be afraid to make mistakes; each error is a learning opportunity that brings you one step closer to mastery.

Incorporate writing into your practice routine. Start a journal in German, write letters to friends, or participate in online forums and social media groups. These activities will help you think in German and apply the case system in varied contexts. Regular writing practice enhances your ability to construct grammatically correct sentences and improves your overall fluency.

Remember, mastering the German case system is a journey, not a destination. Continue to practice, seek out new learning materials, and don't hesitate to revisit challenging topics. The companion workbook and online resources are excellent tools to aid in your continued study.

Finally, I want to acknowledge the effort and dedication you've shown by working through this book. Learning German grammar is no small feat, but with persistence and practice, you will achieve proficiency. Keep pushing forward, and trust in your ability to master the German case system. Viel Erfolg auf deiner Reise!

As an added bonus, this chapter does come with some practice exercises, too. This time, however, they aren't separated out by the cases used or the grammatical structures that are used. These exercises require you to apply the vast amount of information from throughout this book and show me (and yourself) that you are indeed a master of the German case system.

Consider this chapter in the workbook and in the online materials as your final exam. You can try to do it without any notes or you can make it an open book exam. I'll leave that part up to you.

Extra materials for this chapter:
https://www.germanwithantrim.com/mastering-cases/

Additional Resources

As a quick reminder, there are a ton of additional resources available to you. Some are free and are a bonus that goes with the purchase of this book. Others are paid add-ons meant to enhance your experience. You can find each of those items listed below.

Deutschlerner Club:
Every lesson within this book is also available as part of Herr Antrim's Deutschlerner Club. This is an online subscription that grants you access to the A1 and A2 courses as well as lessons Herr Antrim uploads to his YouTube channel. Since the publication of this book there is now an additional course in the Deutschlerner Club designed to follow this book and provide even more support for your mastery of the German case system. You can get free samples of the Deutschlerner Club or join here:
https://www.germanwithantrim.com/store/

Companion Workbook:
Practice what you learn in this book with worksheets and answer keys designed to follow this book exactly so you make sure you actually master everything you learn here. Look for Herr Antrim's companion workbook wherever books are sold.

Online Flashcards:
Flashcards that include example sentences with audio, verb lists, and general vocabulary covered throughout this book can be found in the flashcards folder at
https://www.germanwithantrim.com/mastering-cases/

These flashcards are built on the Anki platform, but should be easy to import into your flashcard app of choice.

Email Support:
I love hearing from my fans (and occasionally from my critics). If you have questions about the book, how to use it to get the best results, where to find any of the materials, or anything you want to know, send me an email at info@germanwithantrim.com

If you find an error in these pages, please send me an email about that too. I want this book to be the best resource it can be for German learners and while I did have a few native speakers read through this book before publishing it, there is always a chance that something slipped by the censors.

Book Reviews:
Thank you for choosing this book. If you have some spare time, consider writing a review online. If you want to write a review on Amazon, you can use this link: https://www.germanwithantrim.com/mastering-cases-review/

Herr Antrim's Newsletter
If you would like to receive free German lessons, motivation and tips emailed to you on a regular basis, join Herr Antrim's newsletter at
https://www.germanwithantrim.com/

Quick Reference German Grammar Guide

Der-Words & Adjective Endings

	Masculine	Feminine	Neuter	Plural
Nom	der + -e	die + -e	das + -e	die + -en
Acc	den + -en	die + -e	das + -e	die + -en
Dat	dem + -en	der + -en	dem + -en	den + -en (n)
Gen	des + -en (s)	der + -en	des + -en (s)	der + -en

Ein-Words & Adjective Endings

	Masculine	Feminine	Neuter	Plural
Nom	ein + -er	eine + -e	ein + -es	(k)eine + -en
Acc	einen + -en	eine + -e	ein + -es	(k)eine + -en
Dat	einem + -en	einer + -en	einem + -en	(k)einen + -en (n)
Gen	eines + -en (s)	einer + -en	eines + -en (s)	(k)einer + -en

Unpreceded Adjective Endings

	Masculine	Feminine	Neuter	Plural
Nom	--- + -er	--- + -e	--- + -es	--- + -e
Acc	--- + -en	--- + -e	--- + -es	--- + -e
Dat	--- + -em	--- + -er	--- + -em	--- + -en (n)
Gen	--- + -en (s)	--- + -er	--- + -en (s)	--- + -er

177

Personal Pronouns

Nominative	Accusative	Dative	English
ich	mich	mir	I - me
du	dich	dir	you - you
er	ihn	ihm	he - him
sie	sie	ihr	she - her
es	es	ihm	it - it
wir	uns	uns	we - us
ihr	euch	euch	you - you
sie	sie	ihnen	they - them
Sie	Sie	Ihnen	you - you

Reflexive Pronouns

Nominative	Accusative	Dative	English
ich	mich	mir	I - myself
du	dich	dir	you - yourself
er, sie, es	sich		he, she, it - himself, herself, itself
wir	uns		we - ourselves
ihr	euch		you - yourself
sie, Sie	sich		they, you - themselves, yourself

Demonstrative/Relative Pronouns

	Masculine	Feminine	Neuter	Plural
Nom	der	die	das	die
Acc	den	die	das	die
Dat	dem	der	dem	denen
Gen	dessen	deren	dessen	deren

German Colors

German	English	German	English
weiß	white	schwarz	black
grau	grey	rot	red
orange	orange	gelb	yellow
grün	green	blau	blue
lila (violett)	purple (violet)	rosa	pink
braun	brown	beige	beige
silber	silver	gold	gold
hell	light (pastel)	dunkel	dark
bunt	colorful	farblos	colorless

Weak Nouns

Affe - Affen monkey	**Architekt - Architekten** architect	**Bauer - Bauern** farmer
Bayer - Bayern Bavarian man	**Biologe - Biologen** biologist	**Brite - Briten** British man
Buchstabe - Buchstaben letter (of alphabet)	**Bulgare - Bulgaren** Bulgarian	**Bulle - Bullen** bull, cop (slang)
Bursche - Burschen boy, lad	**Bär - Bären** bear	**Bürokrat - Bürokraten** bureaucrat
Chinese - Chinesen Chinese man	**Demokrat - Demokraten** democrat	**Diplomat - Diplomaten** diplomat
Däne - Dänen Danish man	**Elefant - Elefanten** elephant	**Este - Sten** Estonian man
Experte - Experten expert	**Finne - Finnen** Finnish man	**Fotograf - Fotografen** photographer
Franzose - Frazosen French man	**Fürst - Fürsten** prince	**Graf - Grafen** count (nobility)
Grieche - Griechen Greek man	**Hase - Hasen** hare	**Held - Helden** hero
Herr - Herren man, gentleman	**Ire - Iren** Irish man	**Journalist - Journalisten** journalist
Jude - Juden Jew	**Junge - Jungen** boy	**Katholik - Katholiken** Catholic

Weak Nouns Continued

Knabe - Knaben boy, lad	Kollege - Kollegen colleague	Komponist - Komponisten composer
Kroate - Kroaten Croatian man	Kunde - Kunden customer	Lette - Letten Latvian man
Löwe - Löwen lion	Mensch - Menschen human being	Monarch - Monarchen monarch
Monegasse - Monegassen Monegasque man	Nachbar - Nachbarn neighbor	Name - Namen name
Narr - Narren fool	Neffe - Neffen nephew	Oberst - Obersten colonel
Pilosoph - Philosophen philiosopher	Pole - Polen Polish man	Polizist - Polizisten police officer
Prinz - Prinzen prince	Präsident - Präsidenten president	Rumäne - Rumänen Romanian man
Russe - Russen Russian man	Schotte - Schotten Scottish man	Schwede - Schweden Swedish man
Sklave - Sklaven slave	Slowake - Slowaken Slovakian man	Slowene - Slowenen Slovenian man
Soziologe - Soziologen sociologist	Student - Studenten student	Tscheche - Tschechen Czech man
Türke - Türken Turkish man	Zeuge - Zeugen witness	

Question Words

German Question Word	English Question Word	German Example	English Example
wer	who	Wer ist das?	Who is that?
wen	whom (accusative)	Wen lädst du ein?	Whom are you inviting?
wem	whom (dative)	Wem schickst du die Karte?	Whom are you sending the card?
wessen	whose	Wessen Auto steht vor dem Haus?	Whose car is standing in front of the house?
wo	where	Wo wohnst du?	Where do you live?
woher	from where	Woher kommst du?	Where are you from?
wohin	to where	Wohin fahren wir morgen?	Where are we driving tomorrow?
wie	how	Wie groß bist du?	How tall are you?
wie viel	how much	Wie viel kostet das?	How much does this cost?
wie viele	how many	Wie viele Geschenke kaufst du?	How many gifts are you buying?
welcher	which	Welche Farbe hat dein Hemd?	Which collor is your shirt?
was für ein	what kind of	Was für ein Auto fährst du?	What kind of a car do you drive?

Accusative Prepositions

bis - until	durch - through	entlang - along	für - for
gegen - against, around (time)	ohne - without	um - around, at (time)	wider - against, contra

Dative Prepositions

aus - out of, from	außer - except, besides, in addition to	bei - at, near, with
gegenüber - across from	mit - with	nach - after, to
seit - since, for (time)	von - from	zu - to, at

Two-Way Prepositions

an - on (vertical)	auf - on (horizontal)	hinter - behind
in - in	neben - next to, beside	über - above, over
unter - under	vor - in front of, before	zwischen - between

Genitive Prepositions

anlässlich - on the occasion of	anstatt - instead of	aufgrund - on the basis of, because of	außerhalb - outside of
bezüglich - with regard to	diesseits - this side of	innerhalb - inside of	jenseits - on the other side of
kraft - by virtue of	laut - according to	oberhalb - above	seitens - on the side of
trotz - despite, in spite of	unterhalb - under	wegen - because of	während - during

Dative Verbs

ähneln - to resemble	antworten - to answer	applaudieren - to applaud
auffallen - to stand out	ausweichen - to evade	befehlen - to order, command
begegnen - to meet someone	beistehen - to stand by, support	danken - to thank
dienen - to serve	drohen - to threaten	einfallen - to come to mind, think of something
entgegnen - to reply, retort	erlauben - to allow, permit	erscheinen - to appear
fehlen - to be missing	folgen - to follow	gefallen - to please
gehorchen - to obey	gehören - to belong to	gelingen - to succeed
genügen - to suffice, be enough	geschehen - to happen, occur	glauben - to believe
gleichen - to closely resemble	glücken - to succeed, work out	gratulieren - to congratulate
helfen - to help	lauschen - to eavesdrop, listen in	munden - to taste good
passen - to fit	passieren - to happen	raten - to advise
schaden - to damage, do harm	schmecken - to taste (good)	schmeicheln - to flatter
sich näher - to approach, draw near to	trauen - to trust	weh/leid tun - to hurt, cause pain / to apologize
vertrauen - to trust, confide in, rely on	weichen - to yield to, make way for	widersprechen - to contradict, gainsay
winken - to wave		

Present Tense Conjugation of Regular Verbs

German	Endings	machen	gehen	lernen
English	-	to do	to go	to learn
ich	-e	mache	gehe	lerne
du	-st	machst	gehst	lernst
er, sie, es	-t	macht	geht	lernt
wir	-en	machen	gehen	lernen
ihr	-t	macht	geht	lernt
sie, Sie	-en	machen	gehen	lernen
German	kennen	kommen	sammeln	wandern
English	to know (nouns)	to come	to collect	to hike
ich	kenne	komme	samm(e)le	wand(e)re
du	kennst	kommst	sammelst	wanderst
er, sie, es	kennt	kommt	sammelt	wandert
wir	kennen	kommen	sammeln	wandern
ihr	kennt	kommt	sammelt	wandert
sie, Sie	kennen	kommen	sammeln	wandern

Present Tense Conjugation of Regular Verbs Continued

German	reisen	hassen	heißen	sitzen
English	to travel	to hate	to be called	to sit
ich	reise	hasse	heiße	sitze
du	reist	hasst	heißt	sitzt
er, sie, es	reist	hasst	heißt	sitzt
wir	reisen	hassen	heißen	sitzen
ihr	reist	hasst	heißt	sitzt
sie, Sie	reisen	hassen	heißen	sitzen
German	reden	reiten	atmen	zeichnen
English	to talk	to ride	to breathe	to draw
ich	rede	reite	atme	zeichne
du	redest	reitest	atmest	zeichnest
er, sie, es	redet	reitet	atmet	zeichnet
wir	reden	reiten	atmen	zeichnen
ihr	redet	reitet	atmet	zeichnet
sie, Sie	reden	reiten	atmen	zeichnen

Present Tense Conjugation of Modal Verbs + werden

German	dürfen	können	mögen	möchten
English	may, to be allowed to	can, to be able to	to like	would like
ich	darf	kann	mag	möchte
du	darfst	kannst	magst	möchtest
er, sie, es	darf	kann	mag	möchte
wir	dürfen	können	mögen	möchten
ihr	dürft	könnt	mögt	möchtet
sie, Sie	dürfen	können	mögen	möchten
German	müssen	sollen	wollen	werden
English	must, to have to	should, to be supposed to	to want	will (future tense)
ich	muss	soll	will	werde
du	musst	sollst	willst	wirst
er, sie, es	muss	soll	will	wird
wir	müssen	sollen	wollen	werden
ihr	müsst	sollt	wollt	werdet
sie, Sie	müssen	sollen	wollen	werden

Present Tense Conjugation of Common Irregular Verbs

German	sein	haben	wissen	nehmen
English	to be	to have	to know (facts)	to take
ich	bin	habe	weiß	nehme
du	bist	hast	weißt	nimmst
er, sie, es	ist	hat	weiß	nimmt
wir	sind	haben	wissen	nehmen
ihr	seid	habt	wisst	nehmt
sie, Sie	sind	haben	wissen	nehmen

Stem-Changing Verbs
Present Tense Conjugation Examples

German	fahren	geben	sehen
English	to drive	to give	to see
ich	fahre	gebe	sehe
du	fährst	gibst	siehst
er, sie, es	fährt	gibt	sieht
wir	fahren	geben	sehen
ihr	fahrt	gebt	seht
sie, Sie	fahren	geben	sehen

Stem-Changing Verbs Lists

a-ä

backen - to bake	braten - to grill, fry, roast	fahren - to drive	fallen - to fall
fangen - to catch	graben - to dig	halten - to stop, hold	laden - to load
laufen - to run	lassen - to let, leave	raten - to advise	schlafen - to sleep
schlagen - to hit, strike	tragen - to wear, carry	wachsen - to grow	waschen - to wash

e-i

bergen - to recover, save	bersten - to burst	brechen - to break	erschrecken - to scare
(fr)essen - to eat	flechten - to braid	geben - to give	gelten - to be valid
helfen - to help	messen - to measure	nehmen - to take	quellen - to gush, well up
schmelzen - to melt	schwellen - to swell	sprechen - to speak	stechen - to stab, prick
sterben - to die	treffen - to meet	treten - to step	verbergen - to hide, disguise
verderben - to decay, spoil	vergessen - to forget	werben - to advertise	werfen - to throw

e-ie

* empfehlen - to recommend	*Without the prefix emp-, the verb "fehlen" is regular. The stem change also occurs with the prefix be-.
** geschehen - to happen	
sehen - to see	**This verb is almost exclusively used in the er, sie, es form. The other forms are listed here for conjugation practice purposes, but aren't really ever needed.
stehlen - to steal	

Separable Prefixes

ab-	an-	auf-	aus-	auseinander-
bei-	da-	dabei-	dar-	daran-
dazwischen-	ein-	empor-	entgegen-	entlang-
entzwei-	fehl-	fern-	fest-	fort-
frei-	gegenüber-	gleich-	heim-	her-
herab-	heran-	herauf-	heraus-	herbei-
herein-	herum-	herunter-	hervor-	herüber-
hin-	hinab-	hinauf-	hinaus-	hinein-
hinterher-	hinunter-	hinweg-	hinzu-	hoch-
los-	mit-	nach-	nebenher-	nieder-
statt-	vor-	voran-	voraus-	vorbei-
vorweg-	vorüber-	weg-	weiter-	zu-
zurecht-	zurück-	zusammen-		

Inseparable Prefixes

be-	ent-	emp-	er-
ge-	miss-	ver-	zer-

Overview of German Tenses

Tense	German Example	English Example
Präsens - Present	Ich mache das.	I do (am doing) that.
Perfekt - Present Perfect	Ich habe das gemacht.	I did that. (I have done that.)
Präteritum - Simple Past	Ich machte das.	I did that. (I have done that.)
Plusquamperfekt - Past Perfect	Ich hatte das gemacht.	I had done that. (I had been doing that.)
Futur 1 - Future	Ich werde das machen.	I will do that. (I will be doing that.)
Futur 2 - Future Perfect	Ich werde das gemacht haben.	I will have done that. (I will have been doing that.)
Präsens - Present	Der Junge geht ins Geschäft.	The boy goes into the store. (The boy is going into the store.)
Perfekt - Present Perfect	Der Junge ist ins Geschäft gegangen.	The boy went into the store. (The boy was going into the store.)
Präteritum - Simple Past	Der Junge ging ins Geschäft.	The boy went into the store. (The boy was going into the store.)
Plusquamperfekt - Past Perfect	Der Junge war ins Geschäft gegangen.	The boy had gone into the store. (The boy had been going into the store.)
Futur 1 - Future	Der Junge wird ins Geschäft gehen.	The boy will go into the store. (The boy will be going into the store.)
Futur 2 - Future Perfect	Der Junge wird ins Geschäft gegangen sein.	The boy will have gone into the store. (The boy will have been going into the store.)

Tense	German Example	English Example
Präsens - Present	Das Kind muss nach Hause gehen.	The child has to go home. (The child is having to go home.)
Perfekt - Present Perfect	Das Kind hat nach Hause gehen müssen.	The child had to go home. (The child has had to go home.)
Präteritum - Simple Past	Das Kind musste nach Hause gehen.	The child had to go home. (The child has had to go home.)
Plusquamperfekt - Past Perfect	Das Kind hatte nach Hause gehen müssen.	The child had had to go home. (The child had been having to go home.)
Futur 1 - Future	Das Kind wird nach Hause gehen müssen.	The child will have to go home. (The child will be having to go home.)
Futur 2 - Future Perfect	Das Kind wird nach Hause sein gehen müssen.	The child will have had to go home. (The child will have been having to go home.)

Irregular Past Tense Verb Patterns

a-u-a

Infinitiv	Präteritum	Partizip 2	Englisch
fahren	fuhr	gefahren	to drive
laden	lud	geladen	to load
schlagen	schlug	geschlagen	to hit, strike
tragen	trug	getragen	to carry
waschen	wusch	gewaschen	to wash

ei-ie-ie

Infinitiv	Präteritum	Partizip 2	Englisch
bleiben	blieb	geblieben	to stay, remain
entscheiden	entschied	entschieden	to decide
leihen	lieh	geliehen	to loan, lend
scheinen	schien	geschienen	to shine
schreien	schrie	geschrien	to scream
schreiben	schrieb	geschrieben	to write
steigen	stieg	gestiegen	to climb

ei-ie-ie (Exceptions)

Infinitiv	Präteritum	Partizip 2	Englisch
heißen	hieß	geheißen	to be called
reiten	ritt	geritten	to ride
schneiden	schnitt	geschnitten	to cut

ie-o-o

Infinitiv	Präteritum	Partizip 2	Englisch
biegen	bog	gebogen	to bend, kneel
bieten	bot	geboten	to offer, provide
fliegen	flog	geflogen	to fly
schießen	schoss	geschossen	to shoot
schließen	schloss	geschlossen	to close, shut
verlieren	verlor	verloren	to lose
ziehen	zog	gezogen	to pull

ie-o-o (Exceptions)

Infinitiv	Präteritum	Partizip 2	Englisch
liegen	lag	gelegen	to lie, be located

i-a-o

Infinitiv	Präteritum	Partizip 2	Englisch
beginnen	begann	begonnen	to begin
gewinnen	gewann	gewonnen	to win
schwimmen	schwamm	geschwommen	to swim
spinnen	spann	gesponnen	to spin
sprechen	sprach	gesprochen	to speak
sterben	starb	gestorben	to die
treffen	traf	getroffen	to meet
werfen	warf	geworfen	to throw
brechen	brach	gebrochen	to break
helfen	half	geholfen	to help
nehmen	nahm	genommen	to take

i-a-u

Infinitiv	Präteritum	Partizip 2	Englisch
finden	fand	gefunden	to find
klingen	klang	geklungen	to sound, ring
singen	sang	gesungen	to sing
trinken	trank	getrunken	to drink

194

i-a-e

Infinitiv	Präteritum	Partizip 2	Englisch
bitten	bat	gebeten	to ask, request
essen	aß	gegessen	to eat
geben	gab	gegeben	to give
lesen	las	gelesen	to read
sehen	sah	gesehen	to see
treten	trat	getreten	to step, kick
sitzen	saß	gesessen	to sit
liegen	lag	gelegen	to lie
vergessen	vergaß	vergessen	to forget

sein

Infinitiv	Präteritum	Partizip 2	Englisch
sein	war	gewesen	to be

X-Y-X

Infinitiv	Präteritum	Partizip 2	Englisch
laufen	lief	gelaufen	to run
heißen	hieß	geheißen	to be called
rufen	rief	gerufen	to call, yell
fangen	fing	gefangen	to catch
hängen	hing	gehangen	to hang

Special Verbs

Infinitiv	Präteritum	Partizip 2	Englisch
gehen	ging	gegangen	to go
kommen	kam	gekommen	to come
stehen	stand	gestanden	to stand
tun	tat	getan	to do
werden	wurde	geworden	to become

Reflexive Verbs

Getting Ready for the Day Verbs

sich abtrocknen - to dry oneself off	sich (etwas) anziehen - to put (something) on
sich ausziehen - to get undressed	sich baden - to bathe
sich die Haare bürsten - to brush one's hair	sich beeilen - to hurry
sich duschen - to shower	sich die Haare föhnen - to blow dry one's hair
sich die Haare kämmen - to comb one's hair	sich die Zähne putzen - to brush one's teeth
sich (etwas) rasieren - to shave (something)	sich schminken - to put on makeup
sich strecken - to stretch	soch umziehen - to get dressed
sich (etwas) waschen - to wash (one's something)	

Angry Verbs

sich ärgern - to get angry/upset	sich aufregen - to get upset

Getting Sick & Getting Better Verbs

sich ausruhen - to rest	sich das Bein brechen - to break one's leg
sich erholen - to recover	sich erkälten - to get sick (with a cold)
sich krank/wohl fühlen - to feel sick/well	sich verletzen - to get hurt

hin or no hin

sich legen - to lay down	sich hinlegen - to lay down
sich setzen - to sit down	sich hinsetzen - to sit down

Verbs that aren't usually reflexive, but can be

sich etwas kaufen - to buy oneself something	sich etwas kochen - to cook oneself something
sich fragen - to wonder	

Relationship Verbs

sich entschuldigen - to excuse oneself, apologize	sich treffen - to meet
sich trennen von - to break up with	sich unterhalten - to converse
sich verlieben in - to fall in love with	sich verstehen - to get along

197

Prepositions Matter

sich bewerben um - to apply for	sich entscheiden für - to decide on
sich erkundigen nach - to inquire about	sich freuen - to be happy/glad
sich freuen auf - to look forward to	sich freuen über - to be happy about
sich fürchten vor - to be afraid of	sich gewöhnen an - to get used to
sich interessieren für - to be interested in	sich konzentrieren auf - to concentrate on
sich kümmern um - to take care of	sich vorbereiten auf - to prepare for

I'm thinking...

sich erinnern - to remember	sich überlegen - to consider, think about
sich vorstellen - to introduce oneself	sich etwas vorstellen - to imagine something
sich etwas wünschen - to wish for something	sich wundern - to be amazed, surprised

Miscellaneous

sich etwas anhören - to listen to something	sich etwas ansehen - to look at something, watch something
sich benehmen - to behave	sich etwas leisten - to afford something

Most Common Adjectives
Comparative & Superlative Forms

Positive	Comparative	Superlative	English
arm	ärmer	am ärmsten	poor
ausgeruht	ausgeruhter	am ausgeruhtesten	relaxed
bekannt	bekannter	am bekanntesten	famous
bequem	bequemer	am bequemsten	comfortable
billig	billiger	am billigsten	cheap
breit	breiter	am breitesten	wide
bunt	bunter	am buntesten	colorful
böse	böser	am bösesten	evil
dick	dicker	am dicksten	fat
dumm	dümmer	am dümmsten	dumb
dunkel	dunkler	am dunkelsten	dark
dünn	dünner	am dünnsten	thin
ehrlich	ehrlicher	am ehrlichsten	sincere
einfach	einfacher	am einfachsten	simple
elegant	eleganter	am elegantesten	elegant
empfindlich	empfindlicher	am empfindlichsten	sensitive
eng	enger	am engsten	narrow
entspannt	entspannter	am entspanntesten	calm
ernst	ernster	am ernstesten	serious
falsch	falscher	am falschesten	false
faul	fauler	am faulsten	lazy

Positive	Comparative	Superlative	English
fest	fester	am festesten	solid
flach	flacher	am flachsten	flat
fleißig	fleißiger	am fleißigsten	hard-working
freigebig	freigebiger	am freigebigsten	generous
freundlich	freundlicher	am freundlichsten	friendly
froh	froher	am frohsten	happy, glad
fröhlich	fröhlicher	am fröhlichsten	cheerful
früh	früher	am frühsten	early
geduldig	geduldiger	am geduldigsten	patient
gefährlich	gefährlicher	am gefährlichsten	dangerous
geizig	geiziger	am geizigsten	stingy
gemütlich	gemütlicher	am gemütlichsten	comfortable, cozy
gerade	gerader	am geradesten	straight
geschickt	geschickter	am geschicktesten	gifted
gestresst	gestresster	am gestresstesten	stressed
gesund	gesünder	am gesündesten	healthy
glatt	glatter / glätter	am glattesten / glättesten	smooth
gleichgültig	gleichgültiger	am gleichgültigsten	indifferent
glücklich	glücklicher	am glücklichsten	happy
groß	größer	am größten	big, large, tall
gut	besser	am besten	good/better/best
hart	härter	am härtesten	hard

Positive	Comparative	Superlative	English
heiß	heißer	am heißesten	hot
hell	heller	am hellsten	light
hoch	höher	am höchsten	high
hungrig	hungriger	am hungrigsten	hungry
hässlich	hässlicher	am hässlichsten	ugly
höflich	höflicher	am höflichsten	polite
hügelig	hügeliger	am hügeligsten	hilly
interessant	interessanter	am interessantesten	interesting
kalt	kälter	am kältesten	cold
klar	klarer	am klarsten	clear
klein	kleiner	am kleinsten	small, short
klug	klüger	am klügsten	smart
krank	kränker	am kränksten	sick
krumm	krummer/ krümmer	am krummsten/ krümmsten	crooked
kurz	kürzer	am kürzesten	short
kühl	kühler	am kühlsten	cool
lang	länger	am längsten	long
langweilig	langweiliger	am langweiligsten	boring
laut	lauter	am lautesten	loud
lebendig	lebendiger	am lebendigsten	alive
lecker	leckerer	am leckersten	delicious
leer	leerer	am leersten	empty

Positive	Comparative	Superlative	English
leicht	leichter	am leichtesten	light
leise	leiser	am leisesten	quiet
locker	lockerer	am lockersten	loose
lustig	lustiger	am lustigsten	funny
mutig	mutiger	am mutigsten	courageous
männlich	männlicher	am männlichsten	manly
möglich	möglicher	am möglichsten	possible, likely
müde	müder	am müdesten	tired
nah	näher	am nächsten	near/nearer/ next
nass	nasser/ nässer	am nassesten/ nässesten	wet
natürlich	natürlicher	am natürlichsten	naturally
negativ	negativer	am negativsten	negative
nervös	nervöser	am nervösesten	nervous
nett	netter	am nettesten	nice
neugierig	neugieriger	am neugierigsten	curious
positiv	positiver	am positivsten	positive
pünktlich	pünktlicher	am pünktlichsten	punctual
rau	rauer	am rausten/rauesten	raw
reich	reicher	am reichsten	rich
richtig	richtiger	am richtigsten	correct
riesig	riesiger	am riesigsten	giant, gigantic

Positive	Comparative	Superlative	English
ruhig	ruhiger	am ruhigsten	quiet
satt	satter	am sattesten	full, satisfied
sauber	sauberer	am saubersten	clean
sauer	saurer	am sauersten	sour
scharf	schärfer	am schärfsten	spicy
schlecht	schlechter	am schlechtesten	bad/worse/worst
schmutzig	schmutziger	am schmutzigsten	dirty
schwach	schwächer	am schwächsten	weak
schwer	schwerer	am schwersten	heavy, dificult, hard
schwierig	schwieriger	am schwierigsten	difficult, hard
schön	schöner	am schönsten	beautiful
sicher	sicherer	am sichersten	secure, safe, certain
sonnig	sonniger	am sonnigsten	sunny
spannend	spannender	am spannendsten	exciting
spitz	spitzer	am spitzesten	sharp
sportlich	sportlicher	am sportlichsten	athletic
spät	später	am spätesten	late
stark	stärker	am stärksten	strong
steil	steiler	am steilsten	steep
stumpf	stumpfer	am stumpfsten	blunt, dull

Positive	Comparative	Superlative	English
sympathisch	sympathischer	am sympathischsten	likable, pleasant
süß	süßer	am süßesten	sweet
teuer	teurer	am teuersten	expensive
tief	tiefer	am tiefsten	deep
tot	toter	am totesten	dead
traurig	trauriger	am traurigsten	sad
trocken	trockener	am trockensten	dry
vernünftig	vernünftiger	am vernünftigsten	reasonable
viel	mehr	am meisten	much/more/most
voll	voller	am vollsten	full
vorsichtig	vorsichtiger	am vorsichtigsten	careful
warm	wärmer	am wärmsten	warm
weiblich	weiblicher	am weiblichsten	feminine
weich	weicher	am weichsten	soft
weit	weiter	am weitesten	far
wenig	weniger	am wenigsten	little/less/least
winzig	winziger	am winzigsten	tiny
wolkig	wolkiger	am wolkigsten	cloudy

About the Author

Levi Antrim, known online as Herr Antrim, has been a dedicated high school German teacher in Edwardsville, Illinois since 2009. With a passion for language education, he has also run the popular YouTube channel "Learn German with Herr Antrim" since 2011, where he provides engaging and accessible German language lessons to a global audience and has gained over 200,000 subscribers.

With a commitment to making language learning enjoyable and effective, Herr Antrim continues to inspire and educate learners worldwide, sharing his expertise and enthusiasm for the German language and culture.

More Books by Herr Antrim

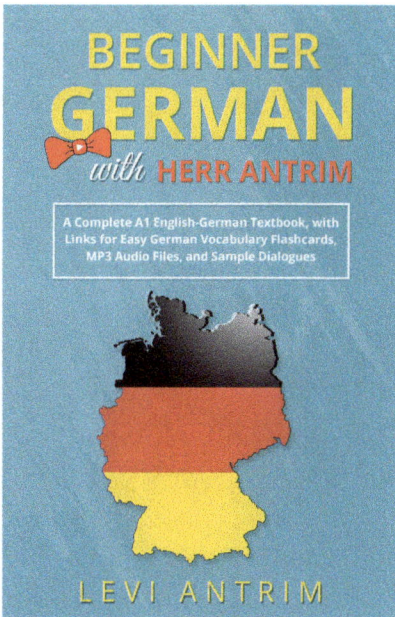

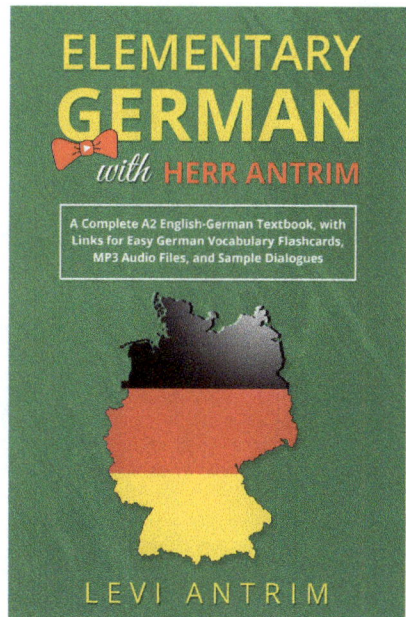

www.ingramcontent.com/pod-product-compliance
Lightning Source LLC
Chambersburg PA
CBHW062132020426
42335CB00013B/1187